How Would You Handle It?

Questions for Teachers to Ask Themselves

Aaron S. Podolner

For my family,
without whom I am nothing
&
for the Golden Apple Scholars of Illinois,
who remind me continuously why I chose to teach.

ISBN: 1482619784
ISBN-13: 978-1482619782

Table of Contents

Foreword

Baseball people, at least those of the veteran stripe, decry that there is an absence of the kind of discussion that used to dominate the dugout, the player's locker rooms and the bars afterwards -- situational baseball. What do you do when this happens? How do you respond when this occurs? How can you best make this action, deflect this occurrence, anticipate and forestall this bad consequence? The old baseball minds would transmit to the up and comers the tips and collective knowledge that could only be acquired from the doing, can only be discussed from the learned, those who have tried and erred and learned and persevered.

The very same can be said of teaching. There are too few opportunities to discuss the situational and the ethical quandaries to which our profession is replete. And you know what? In teaching, the possibilities are multiplied exponentially. The course of a school day, the interaction with dozens if not hundreds of youth during that day, the minutes and the instances, the educative moments and signs far surpass those experienced by eighteen official uniformed ballplayers during a nine-inning game.

University preparation for teaching does well but goes only so far. All of us studied John Dewey, read John Dewey, and wrote papers referring to John Dewey and his blessed ilk that are the cornerstones of contemporary American education. Then, each fall, en masse, thousands of new teachers enter their first classrooms and discover their "Johnny Deweys" -- some from dysfunctional families, some with bright potential but annoying habits, some with learning challenges deep and heartbreaking, some overly bright and easily bored, some reading three grade levels or more below current grade level. And the new teachers so eager and so scared discover as we all discover that the John Dewey we studied has at times little utility in helping us with the Johnny right in front right now needing attention.

These are reasons why Aaron Podolner's accumulated wisdom and perspective has currency and should be attended to carefully. The entire first chapter of one's teaching career can be summed in a blur of what-do-you-do-when-this-happens, and we veterans recall with blush and chuckle how we flopped about and erred left and right before wisdom from the elder down the hall or our own deep reflection got us to the point where we began to make fewer errors the next year than we did the year prior, with each step becoming more assured, accomplished, active.

So reading through what Podolner has put together accelerates the teaching maturation process by using the old school method of talking about teaching! With all that is foisted upon teachers today, it helps to have a trusted voice with a virtual arm around your shoulder suggesting there is a way to consider the endless conundrums teachers face.

And it is good to have Podolner as your guide. Beloved as he is in his profession and in our organization, his credibility stems from his deep humility, his earnest desire to always improve his craft, and from his love of helping the next generation of resilient and inspiring teachers. So take a deep breath, find a comfy spot, begin reading and start talking with your colleagues about how best to engage in this most noble of professions. You have an expert guide to raise questions and offer suggestions.

Best of luck to you in your work with children and always.

Dominic Belmonte
President and CEO
Golden Apple Foundation
Chicago

Introduction

Because I had four classrooms on three different floors, my office consisted of a projector cart on wheels that I rode from class to class like a two-story skateboard. I subsisted on the fuel present only in beginner teachers: an idealistic notion of what I could accomplish and the freedom of being careless with my time. Most days kept me at the school from 7am to 7pm, and I remember once staying at school for eighteen hours.

During that first year, I spent most of my after school time obsessing about what to do the following day. I struggled with decisions regarding everything from what material I should cover to how I could connect with each of my 120 students. Despite all of my planning, teaching was a constant struggle. Every period of the day presented its own challenges, but period five was the hardest. When that group of students walked in, I felt less like a remedial math teacher and more like an inexperienced cowboy riding a bucking bronco.

All of the students in that class were as poor at math as I was at teaching it, and that didn't make for a good combination, particularly with a class scheduled close to lunchtime. Moreover, the classroom was tiny, and the only way to move down a row of seats was to scoot sideways. I could count on my daily anxiety to peak right before that class began. Sometimes it went well, but most days I was incredibly ineffective, and together, we were not moving forward.

It is a sticky day at the end of April. The small room has too many warm bodies, and the students respond by being as uncooperative as possible. With about ten minutes left in class, I notice some slow-motion movement at the back of a row. Jeremy, a quick-talking and excitable young man, is gradually moving his hand towards Tanya, a slow-talking and earnest young woman. I can tell they aren't passing notes, but beyond that, I have no idea what is going on. I continue the explanation of congruent triangles and am relieved when I see Jeremy's hand disappear.

That sense of relief soon vanishes as I realize that Jeremy's hand is under Tanya's shirt and slowly creeping upwards.

At this point in my nascent teaching career, I have two strategies for dealing with misbehavior. One is to get close to Jeremy and by sheer proximity, get him to rethink his actions. The cramped setup rules out that option. The other option is to say something. But what can I say? If I draw attention to him, many of the students will see what is happening, and that will undoubtedly embarrass Tanya. In fact, I don't even know if this act is consensual or an unwanted advance because she doesn't have the opportunity to say "no." While I am thinking about these possibilities and trying to teach at the same time, I see that Jeremy's hand is fully on top of Tanya's breast.

In the end, and to my eternal shame, I do nothing. I wait to be saved by the bell and don't even pull Jeremy or Tanya aside to talk about what happened. I get on my double decker cart and ride off to period six on the other side of the school.

In the days that followed, I realized that I blew it but also sensed that I was totally unprepared for situations like the one between Jeremy and Tanya.

By the end of the year, Jeremy was expelled from the school and Tanya was pregnant. I realize that I probably couldn't have prevented either of those outcomes, but I am aware enough to know that there is a great disparity between saving a student and doing nothing for a student.

It is a different sort of gap that I wish to address in this book of questions for teachers to ask themselves. University-based teacher preparation programs do a fine job of teaching the history and philosophy of education, but too often they leave it to the teaching experience itself to fill in the practical details of teaching. How should you improvise when your lesson doesn't go well? How should you handle situations with students, colleagues and parents that are out of the ordinary? It is no wonder that many teachers comment that they really didn't learn much until they were faced with actual classroom experiences.

The crux of this book is that the worst possible time to think about how you would handle a situation is while it is actually happening. There were countless interactions during my first few years of teaching that I could have managed better if I had thought about them ahead of time. *How Would You Handle It* is the book I wish I had read before I began my teaching career. Although traditional educational philosophy is certainly important, when you are confronted with the extraordinary situations that arise daily in the classroom, you are unlikely to draw on the writings of John Dewey or Horace Mann. Instead, you are apt to pull from internal rather than external resources.

I argue throughout this book that examining your *self* is the most important way to begin preparing yourself for a teaching career. You will take classes that emphasize how different students can be, but teachers also have their own backgrounds and personalities that directly affect their teaching. I ask you to not pretend that we are all the same – instead, I encourage you to be completely honest about what you bring (good and bad) to the classroom.

The first chapter of this book asks you to scrutinize your own **Educational History, Feelings and Philosophy**. Each of us has his or her own past as a student, and those years shaped us in ways that are difficult to articulate. For some, a single interaction in class or with an instructor has long-term effects and for others, the totality of their academic career is most important.

The questions about your feelings are more personal and sensitive. Of the many jobs available to adults, teaching is one that involves putting an incredible amount of one's *self* on display. This makes individual interactions with students, colleagues and parents more intense and emotional. When a student blows up in class, for example, it can take days to fully recover. When it comes to any sort of evaluation, it is rarely easy to hear negative feedback about your teaching, regardless of the source.

Consciously and subconsciously, our educational history and feelings interconnect to make an informal and very personal philosophy of education. Throughout this book, the term philosophy is used as a significantly more informal version of one's thoughts and feelings and not necessarily a coherent part of a comprehensive educational philosophy. It is one thing to reference Piaget or Vygotsky in a philosophy of education paper, but showing mastery of their ideas doesn't necessarily imply that their theories are integrated into a teacher's day-to-day classroom decisions. In my calculation, a personal philosophy of education embodies how one views teaching as a whole, what one sees as his or her role in that process and what one's assumptions are about all of the groups encountered (students, parents, colleagues and administrators).

I've searched but never found a metaphor that totally encapsulates how I view teaching. There are days in the classroom when I feel like a practitioner of Jujitsu – using my students' own force to get them to do what I want rather than applying my own force. On better days, I am a conductor in a symphony of minds. Often, I play the part of a coach doing anything I can to motivate reticent learners. Before school, after school and sometimes between classes, I'm a parent trying to guide my students towards making better choices.

Teachers set out to impart knowledge, maintain a safe environment, and focus instruction on students. But each teacher is guided by her own assumptions about what it means to teach well. For example, I know that my classroom runs more smoothly when I dictate every aspect of our time together. While I appreciate order, I also know a more student-centered classroom may lead to higher-level thinking and learning. Am I willing to trade a little chaos for a better student experience? And what if I *know* they would learn more when they take the lead, but the students' overwhelming preference is for me to tell them exactly what to do? Not only do I need to figure out the way in which my students will learn best, but I also have to know when to overrule their own learning preferences.

Often, the issues you have to navigate require an understanding of your students and whole-class dynamics, and that requires a meaningful relationship between you and them. There is no shortage of authors and public intellectuals who will espouse the importance of teacher-student relationships. I totally agree that students need to know that we care and understand their individual situations, but I think teachers truly need to understand themselves and what that means in terms of relationships with students. Do you tell yourself that you want to be respected by your students but secretly seek adoration, admiration and even love? I do. Would you argue that you don't notice race, for example, when you meet your students? That's unlikely and probably unhealthy, too.

Chapter 2, Relationships With Students will encourage you to contemplate your assumptions about teaching and students. Do you assume that students need to be treated like young adults or growing children? Should you organize your class to teach the value of individual and self-directed persistence or will you present a more flexible and forgiving model that allows the student to develop with natural consequences for bad choices? Whether you realize it or not, these assumptions and more play out in your lessons and individual interactions with students. The more you know about why you are doing what you are doing, the more effectively you can reflect on ways to improve the experience for all students.

Chapter 3, Relationships With Parents discusses how many interactions with parents go beyond what your school requires of you, leaving wide a berth for teacher discretion. Parents are the primary educators of young children and more importantly, parents are critical to the development of self-discipline, ability to focus, intellectual curiosity, self-confidence and an understanding of the relationship between education and future success. Missing these characteristics during formative years for children can present insurmountable obstacles at the middle and high school levels; though it is certainly possible to regenerate a commitment to education. When discussing an underperforming student with a parent, what responsibility should you assume and how much onus belongs with the student? You could do everything a parent asks you to do, but would that necessarily be best for the student? Or for you? There are no permanent answers to these questions, but they are incredibly important to ponder before you can develop meaningful and productive relationships with parents.

Chapter 4, Assumptions About Teaching continues the exploration of your educational opinions and philosophy with simple statements. The aim is to make you a better advocate for your profession and your ideals. Some comments may originate with a community member or a parent, and others may come from a college professor or a politician. You can agree or disagree, but carefully think through your choice. The statements in this section may lead you to do further research on a topic, and that can help justify your classroom choices and increase your ability to articulate them to others. Or you might adjust your approach given new evidence. Either way, everyone gains when teachers carefully analyze all of the issues related to teaching children.

Chapter 5, Would You Rather is derived from my favorite dorm room discussion game (would you rather walk naked through a room full of spiders or drink moldy milk?). These questions will present the dilemmas teachers face in the real world: not a choice between an ideal and an intolerable solution but a choice between two justifiable choices. Teachers tend to be idealists, but sometimes the ideal resolution for a conflict is not available. If you don't like the options available, it could be that you need to reexamine your personal philosophy of education. It may be unfair of me to ask if you would rather have a complete social life OR a successful teaching career. And of course, we would all rather be fulfilled in both areas. But the challenge of choosing between the two, even hypothetically, is an excellent way of determining priorities that may affect other small choices throughout a teaching career.

Chapter 6, What Would You Do If... is a perennial favorite in the workshops and seminars that I conduct for future teachers. They have a thirst for in-class examples that are realistic and typically not presented in traditional teacher preparation programs. You have read about my awkward experience with one student fondling another. What will you do if something stranger happens in your own classroom? It would be impossible to prepare for every crazy classroom situation, but going through these examples, particularly with peers and experienced teachers, will give you at least a preliminary approach to help you through some very difficult situations.

Chapter 7, Conduct of Another Teacher aims to put you in the role of observer and commentator. As you think about whether the actions of these teachers are justifiable, you'll ultimately have to decide what you would do in their places. More important than *what* you would do is *why* you would do it. Will all of your actions match your personal philosophy of education or are there internal contradictions? Is it acceptable to have exceptions to the rules you use to guide your decisions? Finally, if there is a difference between what you believe and what choose to do, how should you handle that discrepancy? These are questions that every teacher should ask himself or herself.

Chapter 8, Difficult Choices presents situations for which multiple teachers can explain his or her actions. The question is how you will explain yours. At this point, you should be able to integrate a significant list of examples that bolster your rationale for the various choices that you make as a teacher. Those decisions may be rooted in your personal thoughts and feelings, but they should also adhere to more overarching assumptions and theories about students and learning.

A warning: If you try to find the section of this book with all the answers, you will be sorely disappointed. While I wish I had thought about many of these issues before I had my own classroom, the notion of one set of correct answers might have been more damaging. What's right for me may not be right for you, and my own thoughts on these questions have changed over the years. I hope they continue to evolve because my students and I will be changing throughout the course of my career. I strongly believe that it is helpful to think about all of the aspects of teaching before a classroom decision is made, but it is also important to reflect afterwards. Essentially, there should be no end to reflection as a teacher. I hope this book is a good beginning of that process for you.

That process takes time, and so should reading this book; if you get through it in one sitting, you probably aren't giving yourself a chance to reflect. These questions are designed to be thought provoking and resistant to easy solutions. Additionally, I worked to keep them as free from bias and any "agenda" as possible. Moreover, any use of the pronoun he or she is purely random. Besides the basic maxim that all teachers need to strive to help all children, there aren't any correct answers, just a lot of equally justifiable courses of action.

Preface

To those considering a career in teaching:

When asked what they want to be when they grow up, very young children generally choose from a small and predictable pool of responses: doctor, lawyer, police officer, fireman, and teacher. Children may pass hundreds of hours watching medical and crime-themed shows on TV, but by the time they graduate high school, they have spent about 10,000 hours watching actual teachers in their own classrooms. We know that TV distorts reality and can't be trusted for a true depiction of any profession. Similarly, watching teachers teach doesn't necessarily reveal the nature of teaching. Unless a teacher does all of her thinking aloud, students don't observe the complex decision-making process that educators go through almost continuously.

Viewing movies may inspire you to become an actor, though the bulk of the work goes on behind the scenes. This is basically the same for teaching which largely involves planning, creating (notes, assignments, tests), and evaluating (students and self). I think the stories I have included in this book can help give you a sense of some of the unusual situations that arise in class and are unlikely to appear on television. Additionally, the book details many of the forces that teachers try to balance as they create lessons and work with young people.

As you read the introduction to each section, picture yourself in the situations. Would you react in a similar or different way? Do you think the stories are exaggerations of life as a teacher, accurate reflections of what teachers have to handle, or an understatement of the issues you may face? How do the stories and struggles described in the book match up with what you know about teaching from real life, TV and movies? Is there something that could happen in a class, or classes, that would make you more or less likely to pursue a career in teaching?

You don't have to answer every question in this book. I do, however, think that it would be beneficial to try out a few from every section. Are you willing to analyze your own educational experience with a critical eye? Are you able to be truthful with yourself about the way your teacher personality will dovetail with the needs of your students? How much of yourself are you willing to compromise for your students, your school, and your career?

Take a look at **Chapter 4, Assumptions About Teaching**. My guess is that you have heard many of these statements. Do you think your responses would be closer to what teachers or non-educators would write? Do educational policy issues interest you, or is the classroom your main focus? Do you expect to get involved with the administrative structure at your school, a professional educational association or the teacher's union (if there is one)? Where do you see the field of education going in the future?

I started to think about teaching when I was a junior in high school. Others make this choice much earlier in life, and there are many people who come to teaching as a second career. Regardless of when you started imagining yourself as a teacher, you'll find out one day that the reality of teaching is profoundly different than the dream. That discovery usually arrives with disappointment as your idealistic vision conflicts with the less-than-inspiring elements of reality. The perpetual struggle among idealism, realism and cynicism is present in every self-aware teacher who aims to make a difference. How do you think you will handle being pulled in those different directions? Will you be able to handle the large difference between what you dreamed you would do every day and what you end up doing?

My last suggestion is to talk openly and honestly with as many classroom teachers as possible. You can use my questions or create your own. Ask them what is hard about their jobs, what difficult decisions they have to make, and what they question about their own teaching. The ones who show a high degree of self-reflection may serve as excellent mentors for you throughout your career.

To Pre-service Teachers

This book was written primarily for you -- every chapter was created to invite reflection on a dimension of teaching. Although I have presented many different ways to think about your future career, I am hesitant to tell you exactly how to use this book. The one method I don't recommend is to sit down and try to power through the whole text in one or several quick readings because there's no way to reflect effectively in such a short period of time.

Beyond that, it's up to you. You could concentrate on just one section or dabble in all of them simultaneously. You can jot down your answers in a journal, online or write directly in the space provided for you in this book. I do believe that you will find it fascinating to revisit your answers throughout your career. How does a response to a question or set of questions change before and after your teacher preparation program, student teaching, your first year and your first ten years?

I have high hopes that you will find a teacher preparation program that serves all of your needs and starts you on a path to become an effective teacher. The focus on educational theory and history may initially seem irrelevant, but your professors can demonstrate how the educational past informs the present and how theory informs practice. You may come up with your own hybrid educational theory, though you'll still have to understand the basics of how children learn at various stages of development. Your professors ultimately want you to be able to look at teaching the way they do, as someone capable of doing research and writing publishable papers. Do not ignore these lessons, but also freely question how research and theory assists teachers with the daily struggles they face.

In addition to my personal stories, the questions included could encourage thought-provoking conversations in your education classes. For example, this **Difficult Choices** scenario might lead to a healthy debate when discussing group work:

Mrs. Nash does group work in class and wants her students to be comfortable and work with their friends (unless this is too much of a distraction).

Mr. Ponce does group work in class and wants the students to be with peers that are outside of their social circles to push their boundaries even if it means they are less comfortable.

Mr. Quinn does group work in class and wants students to be with peers with whom they don't get along so that they learn conflict resolution.

Each teacher has a different justification for his or her design. In class, you can cite what various authors have written about each choice *and* discuss your personal experience with group work as a student. My guess is that you'll ultimately make decisions based on what you learn from experience rather than from what you have read. Your professors (and I) would probably say that you will miss out on growth as a teacher if you only defer to your own experience. One is a very small sample size in your self-study experiment, so looking at the literature for contrasting and confirming points of view can help to expand your awareness of what you are doing and, perhaps, lead you to make some modifications.

More than anything, I suggest you talk to your fellow pre-service teachers. Whether in class, in a dorm room or in some electronic format, a cohort of equally passionate future teachers can be your best asset as you prepare for and begin your teaching career.

To Professors of Education

Educational history and theory are an important part of pre-service teacher education. My intention is to help bridge the gap between what teachers learn from their traditional certification programs and what they say they wished they had talked about before entering the classroom.

The first item our administrators passed out during our new teacher orientation program was Harry Wong's "The First Days of School." This book was my initial window into the tension between theory and practice in education. I quickly scanned over the pages to soothe my anxiety and pick up tips for the classroom. Given that the book has sold over 3.3 million copies, it's obvious that Wong has created something useful that is still lacking in many teacher preparation programs. New teachers have an incredible thirst for *what works,* and he does an excellent job filling part of that void.

How Would You Handle It? gives virtually no answers, and instead focuses on the various challenges that teachers feel when they make decisions. I emphasize *what works for you* rather than just *what works*. Because of this open orientation, it is a great fit for college classrooms. Everything that comes up during discussion can be tied to theory, research or a professor's individual experiences.

Pre-service teachers must thoroughly examine their own experiences as student. This "apprenticeship in education" from kindergarten to senior year of high school is ripe for reflection because it manifests itself in their own choices throughout their career as educators. The first chapter, **Personal Educational History, Feelings and Philosophy**, is a place where they can begin to delve into the connections between their personal past and professional future.

Special education has become an integral part of the preparation for all teachers, and it is a critical piece of the educational process in general. The process of differentiating for students with disabilities can be applied to the "typically" abled student without the formal IEP process. A pre-service teacher may someday have a period 2 class whose needs differ sharply from period 5. She could conceivably create an individualized plan for every student and every class. But is that feasible or even desirable? This is another area in which future teachers need help figuring out what works for them and their students. Because that line is fuzzy, teachers need to grapple honestly with some important questions.

- What type of disabilities do you feel most comfortable accommodating in class? Which ones make you most uncomfortable?
- You have a student in the process of getting an IEP who is struggling to write down assignments and turn them in. That child's parent asks you to take responsibility for checking that student's assignment notebook every day and asking the student personally for the assignment the next day. Would you comply? Why or why not?
- Would you rather have your students' grades more reflective of their efforts (on homework, discussion and projects) or understanding (as shown on exams)?

All programs have some instruction related to diversity, and this book should be an important part of that process. Multiple questions can help make your conversation less didactic and more rooted in the feelings and experiences of your students. For example:

- Do you feel equally comfortable being around men and women? Do you think you'll feel equally comfortable around male and female students? How about overtly gay students, students from other races, and students who dress with styles far outside of the mainstream?
- What would you do if you suspected that a student didn't like you because of your race, religion (or lack thereof), national origin or other physical characteristics?

- What do you think about a teacher of a class other than English who believes that it is important for students to always speak in "Standard" English so that they have as many opportunities in life as possible? In this teacher's class are students who speak Black Vernacular English and students who are English language learners. Every time a student makes a mistake, the teacher corrects the individual publicly or privately.

The questions in this book also can help foster more of a community and familial atmosphere with your undergraduate or graduate students. Teaching is more than a job and studying it should be more than a major. As their professor, you have the opportunity to make your time with them more than just a class. It can be greater than a community of learners; it can be a cohort of people who support each other beyond the end of the semester.

- Describe a bad dream that you have had about teaching. What sorts of fears or insecurities are expressed in this dream? Are they rational or irrational?
- If you could wake up tomorrow with one superpower that would help in your classroom, what would it be?
- What would you do if you have to pass gas and there is no way for you to leave the classroom?

More than anything, a process centered on Socratic questioning is more engaging than one in which pre-service teachers are told what to do and how to do it. An added benefit is that they will undoubtedly come up with their own questions for you and each other. A truly progressive college class is possible if it is driven by what the pre-service teachers want to learn.

Besides conversation starters, I can imagine a few alternative assignments using this book. A metacognitive activity could be to assign all of the questions in a given section and challenge the students to figure out a way to organize them. I foresee a wide range of organizational structures worthy of reflection that will reveal how students view teaching.

Another approach could be a variation on the standard philosophy of education paper. Instead of a lofty and sometimes impractical statement of beliefs, try having your pre-service teachers pick a few questions from each section, answer them in writing, and then reflect on what their own answers mean. Are their choices internally consistent or are they using different sets of rules depending on the situation? Can they connect their choices to theory and research on education, or are they drawing their inspiration from somewhere else? What do their choices and explanations say about their readiness to teach?

To In-Service teachers

You already know how to teach and you have experienced some of the **What if...** scenarios that bedevil new teachers. I predict this book could still be helpful for you because it outlines a way of thinking about teaching that emphasizes reflective practice and multiple perspectives. To a great extent, our teaching style and practice is a reflection of our personalities so it would be patently absurd to argue that there's one way to be a good teacher. Teaching is more of a balancing act between the needs of your students, your own needs and the needs stipulated by various school, state and national policies related to education. Throughout this book, you can ask yourself questions like:

Are you making a decision for yourself or your students? If you are making a choice that primarily benefits yourself (like going home at 4pm instead of 7pm), is that OK? Can you argue that spending more time relaxing is actually better for your students? How will you know if you are prepared enough for the next day? Should you forgive yourself when something doesn't go well?

If you deviate from a school policy related to student behavior (like no eating in class, wearing hats, using music playing devices), you'll have to carefully consider why are you makingthat decision and what the consequences may be. Is it because the rule is difficult to enforce? Would you argue that eating during class makes kids more alert and music helps them learn? Or are you trying to gain their trust by seeming more flexible about school rules? Whatever you decide, it is imperative that your choices are well thought out and justifiable.

If you do teach differently than your colleagues, it's worth reflecting on why that is. Is your alternate method more because of your own preferences or because you think it's better for students or both? If there is a teacher who seems to be more effective than you, is her style worth emulating? What would you try out in the classroom, and what is beyond your comfort zone?

I also warn against the dangers of getting too comfortable in your teaching routine. When you stop reflecting as a teacher, you risk becoming bored with your job and boring to your students. This "autopilot" form of teaching isn't good for anyone.

To school administrators

It would probably be unfair to ask a candidate question 507: Would you rather have the respect of your fellow teachers or your administrators?

Or would it give a better sense of what a candidate would be like in the classroom? Requiring mock lessons can serve this function, and so can asking questions from this book. I feel comfortable saying there are few "correct" answers to my questions, but it may be less true for you because you would prefer them to stay closer to school policy. Nevertheless, questions like the following could offer valuable insight into the candidates' thinking:

- Will you decorate your classroom? If so, how will you do it? Will students contribute to the process? What will the function of decoration be?
- Are there elements of your particular approach to teaching that come from the way your parents or a teacher taught you? And did something serve as a negative model that you want to correct through the

substance and style of your teaching?

- Would you rather give an explanation that is too long and some students get bored or too short and the some students are confused because of a lack of detail?
- Would it bother you more to have a student who hated you but did well academically or a student that loved you but did poorly?

Even without "correct" responses, more nuanced answers probably indicate greater thoughtfulness on the part of the teacher and serve as a more accurate predictor of a new teacher's performance. Once employed, new teachers could still find this book helpful. Many of the questions are very personal, so new hires probably will not feel comfortable publically sharing their responses. They might, however, want to ask questions that arise as they ponder the various sections, particularly the **"What If…"** scenarios. I'm sure they'll want guidance on what to do if a fight breaks out, a student acts sexually aggressive, or they suspect child abuse of various forms. Lastly, the **Difficult Choices** chapter could be useful as they think through their own classroom policies and the implications for students of all learning styles.

To Non-educators

From an outsider's perspective, it must be difficult to get a realistic sense of what teachers do every day. You have your own firsthand experience as a student, but you probably don't know what teachers do before and after class to generate that experience. Many parts of this book speak to the overwhelming complexity of teaching and open a small window into what teachers have to think about. While their weekly contractual hours may not seem more than your average American worker, estimates of actual time teachers spend are far beyond the time spent with students. This book won't account for exactly what's done during this time outside the classroom, but it may give insight into what teachers have to think about, particularly the difficult decisions they make every day. Regardless of the official hours at school or grading and planning at home, teachers think about their jobs for many hours beyond the instructional periods. The tension involved in the very difficult and confusing situations that arise should illuminate the anxiety teachers face and our challenge to determine the best choices for our students.

I also see the questions as particularly interesting for parents with school age children. You can look at some or all of them and think about how *you* would want your child's teacher to respond. Additionally, the questions can give you insight into the struggles the teacher may have gone through in making her decision. This may also create a starting point if you have an issue with something the teacher has done that you do not like or understand.

I highly recommend that you always talk first to the teacher when your child tells you something that happened at school that makes you uncomfortable, or if you learn about some policy or practice that you find disagreeable. I continue to be amazed when parents hear a story (or read a text) from their child and promptly call the department chair or e-mail half of the administration. That may create an immediate sense of satisfaction, but any good administrator would refer you back to the teacher as the first step in dealing with the problem. In all likelihood, the teacher involved has thought about the decision she has made and would be happy to discuss the situation with you.

Let's say that the teacher didn't allow your child to turn in a late assignment. Does she have an official policy about late work? Does it align with the school's policy? Does she ever deviate from the policy, and if so, for what reasons? I think it's perfectly fair to ask a teacher's reasoning for a classroom policy and engage in a discussion about it. Throughout this book, I have argued that teacher decisions must be justifiable and not wantonly applied. Ultimately, you'll have to ask yourself if you are arguing for your child or your child's grade. If the teacher's decision adversely affects your child's grade, but is reasonably justified and equitably applied in the classroom, you should probably accept the teacher's decision

Chapter 1

Personal History, Feelings and Philosophy

What if all expectant parents took a series of early childhood education classes? They would learn what childhood development experts say about pre-school development, do observations of effective parenting and write papers about their own philosophy of parenting. It's hard to imagine that this process would hurt our collective ability to parent, but I don't think it would lead to profound change. A few classes are undoubtedly helpful but they would never compare to a *lifetime* of observing parenting by being parented. Similarly, by the time pre-service teachers reach college, they have at least twelve years of experience as an apprentice in education.

This long-term teacher preparation program called *being a student* forms conscious and unconscious orientations to education that are intertwined with an individual's personality. It is only once you start asking yourself far-ranging and deeply personal questions that you can truly glimpse what you have experienced, who you are, and how it will affect your future students.

I believe that a more reflective teacher is a better teacher; I have seen this transformative process because of the specialized role I play each summer. As an employee of the Golden Apple Foundation of Illinois, I am a reflective seminar leader for the same group of future teachers (called Golden Apple Scholars) for years at a time. They intern in various classes, and we reflect on their experiences together. Through summer institutes, I meet them as college freshmen and follow a group through student teaching and into their first jobs. Elisabeth, Juan, Melissa, Ron, Joyce, Namita, Becky, Joe, and LaJoi began with vastly different talents, though all of them left as better, more reflective teachers.

What I aim for with them is a multiyear version of what regular classroom teachers do: accept students for who they are, nurture individual growth and help them reflect on doing their best -- whatever that may be. Elisabeth arrived with raw talent and has gathered an arsenal of teaching techniques. Juan switched from teaching math to teaching Spanish and leverages his heritage to connect with troubled teens. Melissa started off with exceptional talent like Elisabeth but had to step away from teaching before she returned. Joyce is a force to reckon with but was almost broken by her first job. Ron has his own brand of teaching and a special ability to relate to people of all backgrounds. Becky started off passionate, quiet and small. Four years later, she is still small physically but actually gets bigger when she is in front of a group of students. Joe was always adept at reflecting and helping others to think about their own teaching. He is hardest on himself. LaJoi went on to earn a master's at Harvard and plans on becoming the Secretary of Education.

Each began at one place and ended at another. Some had to learn to teach students who are far different from themselves. Others had trouble teaching kids who look exactly like them. For a few, hearing criticism was the hardest part of teaching. Most had a vision of themselves as teachers that was hard to live up to. And a couple of them, who aren't on that list, quit teaching before they began their careers.

Those who remain are finding their own answers and have learned how to reflect in a meaningful way. While a single path is unlikely to emerge, some consistent *tensions* exert career-long forces on classroom teachers. Take personal vs. professional life, for example. Teachers constantly have to struggle with the extent to which they bring their personal lives into the classroom and how much of their professional lives come home with them. Even if a teacher manages to leave his professional life at school, there is always some version of his *self* that shows up in the classroom. There's nothing wrong with the crossover between the two; it only demands careful thought.

We all know the Greek aphorism "know thyself," but it needs to be modified for teachers; know thyself *in relation to your students*. Most teachers liked school but many students do not -- that basic difference leads to constant conflict when the basic goals of teachers and some students don't align. Effective teachers need to meet students somewhere in the space between those two sets of attitudes towards education, but the important question is where that meeting point is for each student, especially the resistant ones. It's true that there aren't correct answers to the questions in this book, but it's erroneous to conclude that the answers don't matter. Every day and in every way, your own history, feelings and philosophy of education unfold in the classroom. Only you (the teacher) can reflect on what that means.

Personal Educational and History

101. Are you meant to be a teacher? Why do you believe that you are?

102. Are there elements of your particular approach to teaching that come in whole or part from the way your parents or a teacher taught you? Has anything served as a negative model that you want to correct through your teaching style?

103. What do you like about the age group that you want to teach?

104. Have you had any teachers that you didn't like at the time but appreciate in retrospect? What about teachers that you liked at the time but realized later that he or she was ineffective?

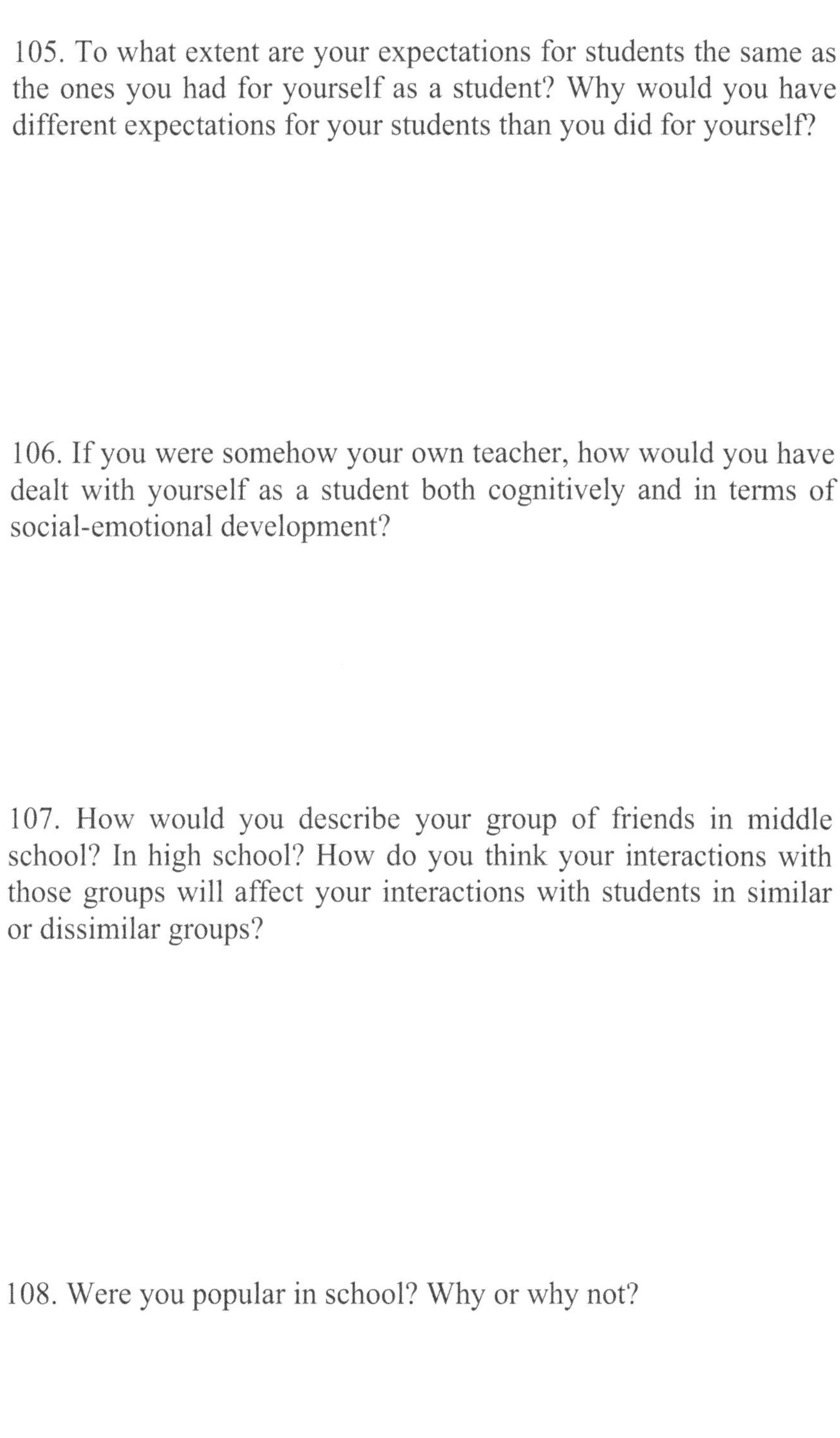

105. To what extent are your expectations for students the same as the ones you had for yourself as a student? Why would you have different expectations for your students than you did for yourself?

106. If you were somehow your own teacher, how would you have dealt with yourself as a student both cognitively and in terms of social-emotional development?

107. How would you describe your group of friends in middle school? In high school? How do you think your interactions with those groups will affect your interactions with students in similar or dissimilar groups?

108. Were you popular in school? Why or why not?

109. Would you ever share your own political or religious beliefs in class? If so, which beliefs do you think are appropriate to share? Which ones are better kept to yourself and why?

110. What was the most exciting academic success of your scholastic career? What was the most significant academic disappointment? How did you react to those experiences? How do those experiences give insight into the way you will react when students have similar successes and disappointments?

111. What was your worst non-academic experience as a student? How does that experience affect you as a teacher? Did you learn anything specific from this experience that would help you if a similar issue arose with one of your students?

112. What was your best non-academic experience as a student? How does that experience affect you as a teacher? Did you learn anything specific from this experience that would help you guide students to write their own success stories?

113. Are you effective at covering up, denying or expanding upon the truth? Would you ever misrepresent the truth to your students? Your colleagues? Your boss? What would warrant an untruth? What about a half-truth? And what about a white lie?

Feelings

114. How well do you take constructive criticism? Are there particular parts of your educational philosophy or style that it would be hard to hear criticized? Why do you think you are sensitive in these areas? Would it matter if it comes from your boss? Another teacher? A student? Are you comfortable providing constructive criticism to your peers?

115. Do you feel equally comfortable being around men and women? Do you think you'll feel equally comfortable around male and female students? How about overtly LGBT students, students from other races, and students who dress with styles far outside of the mainstream?

116. Do you tend to listen or talk more when you converse with friends? Do you feel that as a teacher, you need to work on your reflective listening skills? How about your speaking skills?

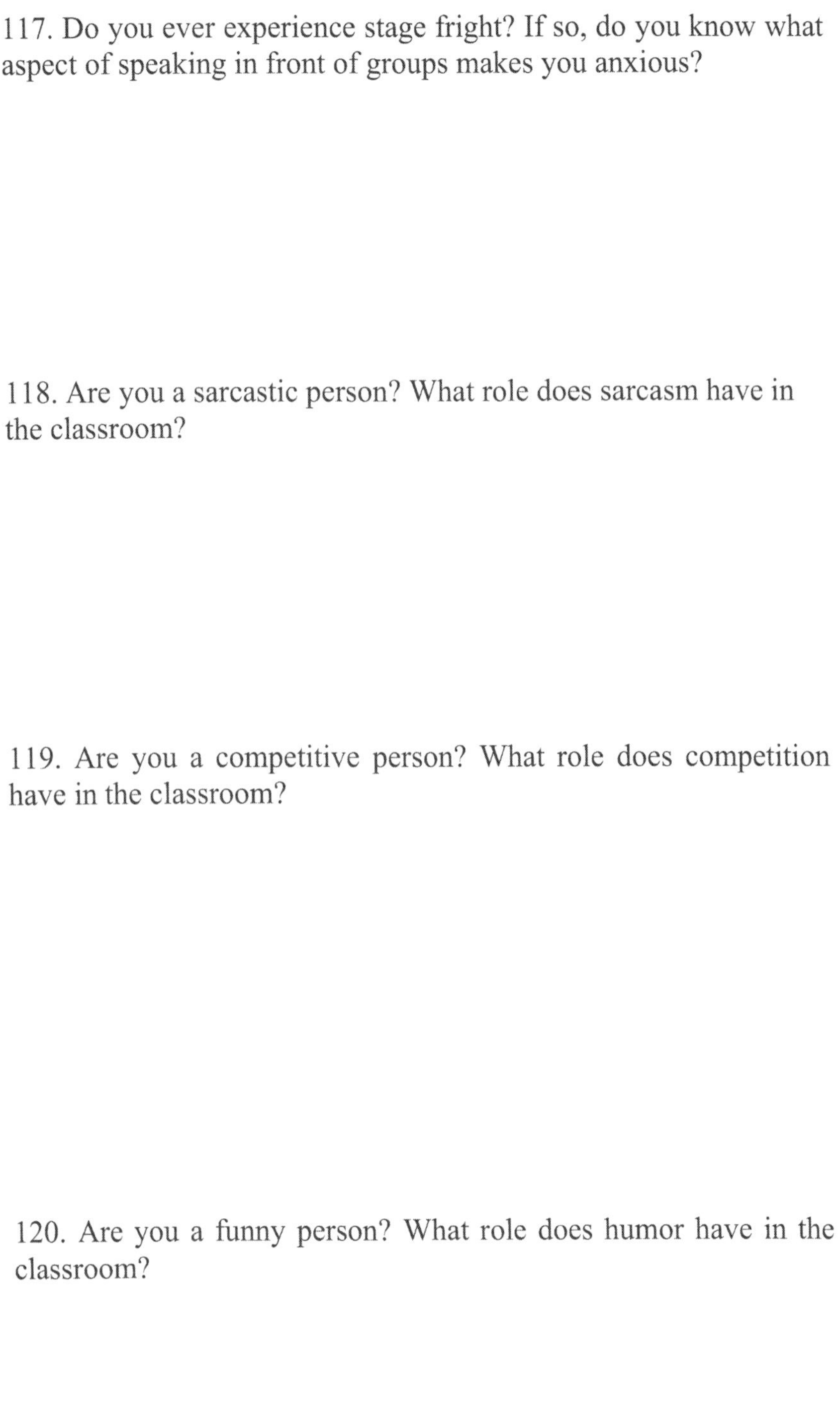

117. Do you ever experience stage fright? If so, do you know what aspect of speaking in front of groups makes you anxious?

118. Are you a sarcastic person? What role does sarcasm have in the classroom?

119. Are you a competitive person? What role does competition have in the classroom?

120. Are you a funny person? What role does humor have in the classroom?

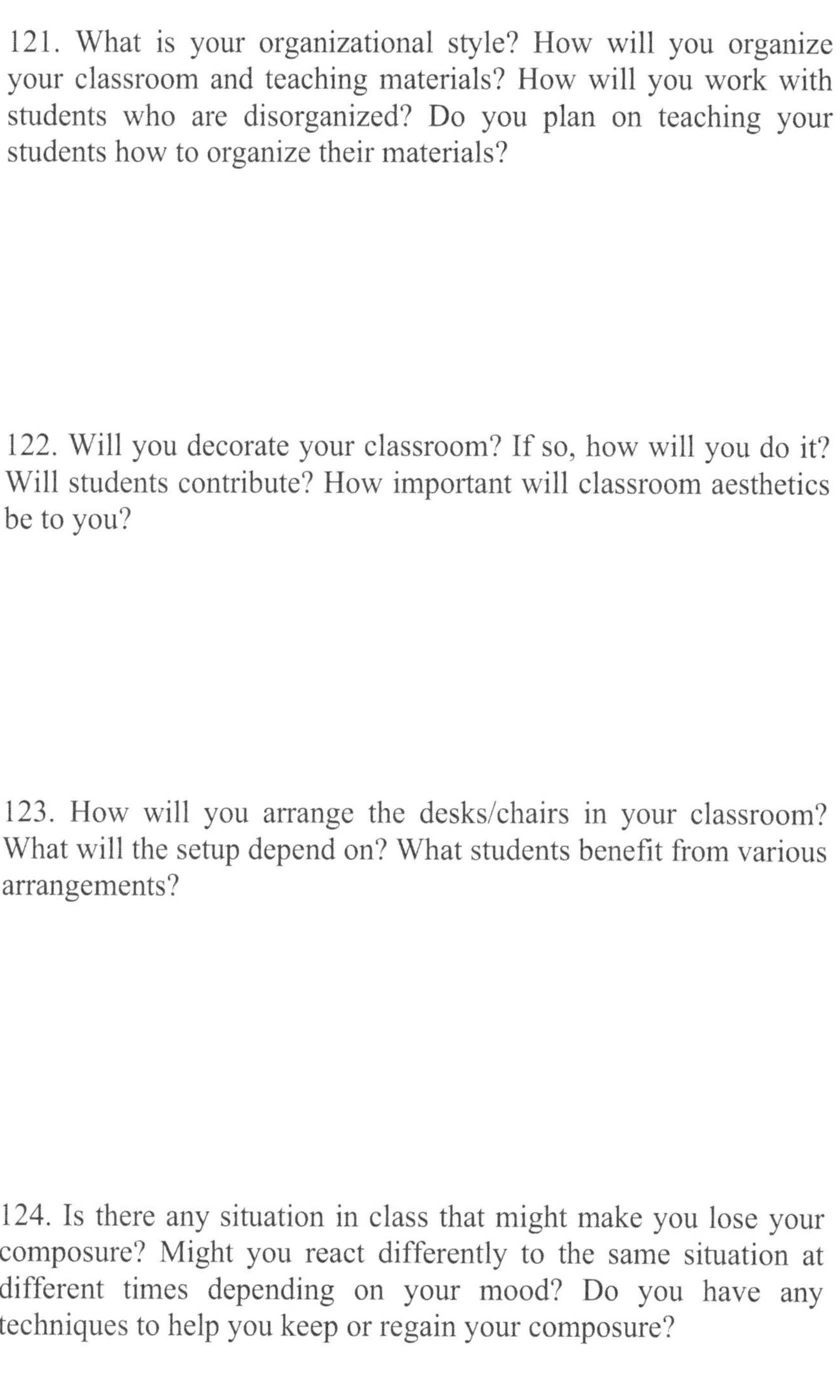

121. What is your organizational style? How will you organize your classroom and teaching materials? How will you work with students who are disorganized? Do you plan on teaching your students how to organize their materials?

122. Will you decorate your classroom? If so, how will you do it? Will students contribute? How important will classroom aesthetics be to you?

123. How will you arrange the desks/chairs in your classroom? What will the setup depend on? What students benefit from various arrangements?

124. Is there any situation in class that might make you lose your composure? Might you react differently to the same situation at different times depending on your mood? Do you have any techniques to help you keep or regain your composure?

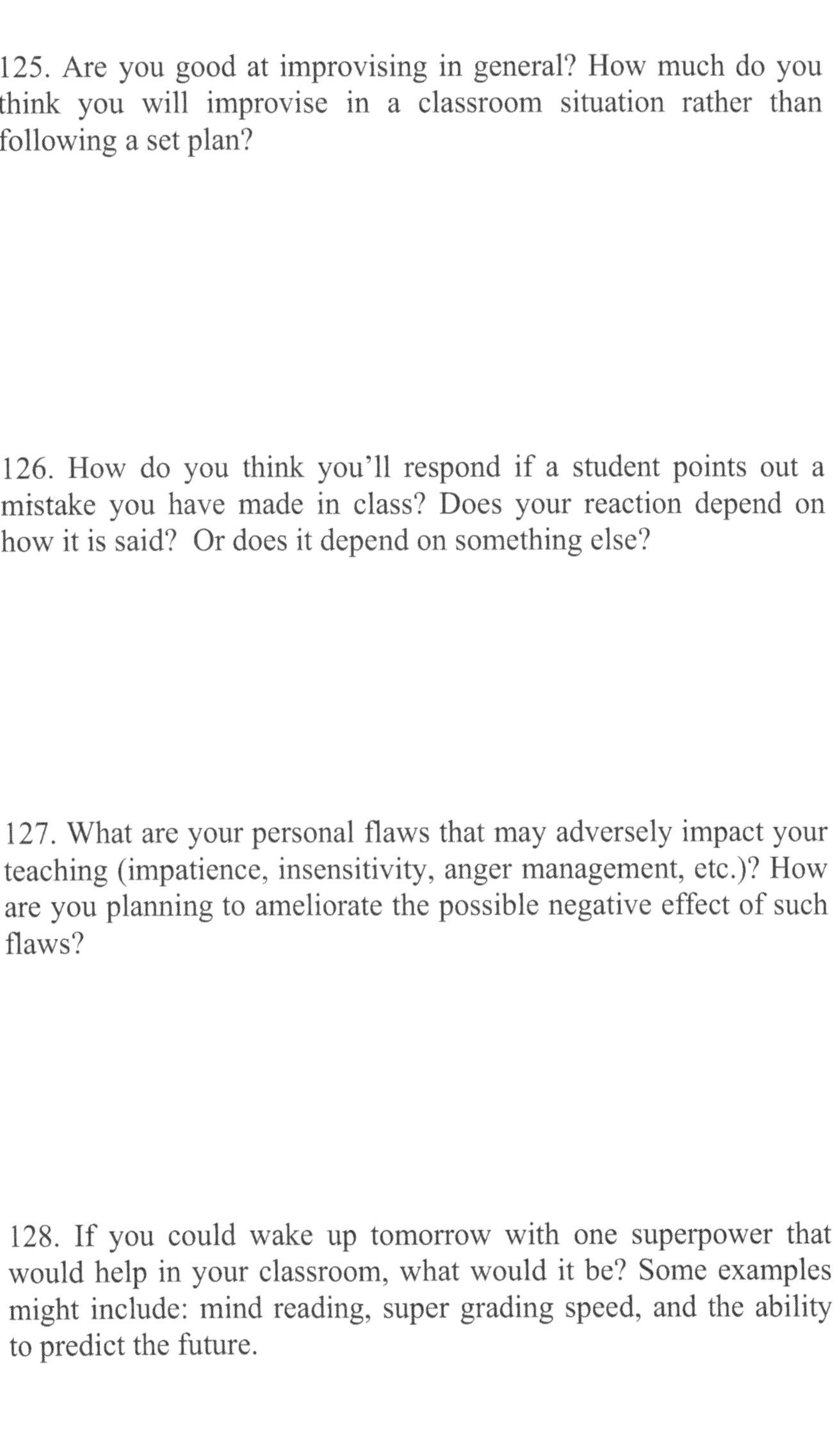

125. Are you good at improvising in general? How much do you think you will improvise in a classroom situation rather than following a set plan?

126. How do you think you'll respond if a student points out a mistake you have made in class? Does your reaction depend on how it is said? Or does it depend on something else?

127. What are your personal flaws that may adversely impact your teaching (impatience, insensitivity, anger management, etc.)? How are you planning to ameliorate the possible negative effect of such flaws?

128. If you could wake up tomorrow with one superpower that would help in your classroom, what would it be? Some examples might include: mind reading, super grading speed, and the ability to predict the future.

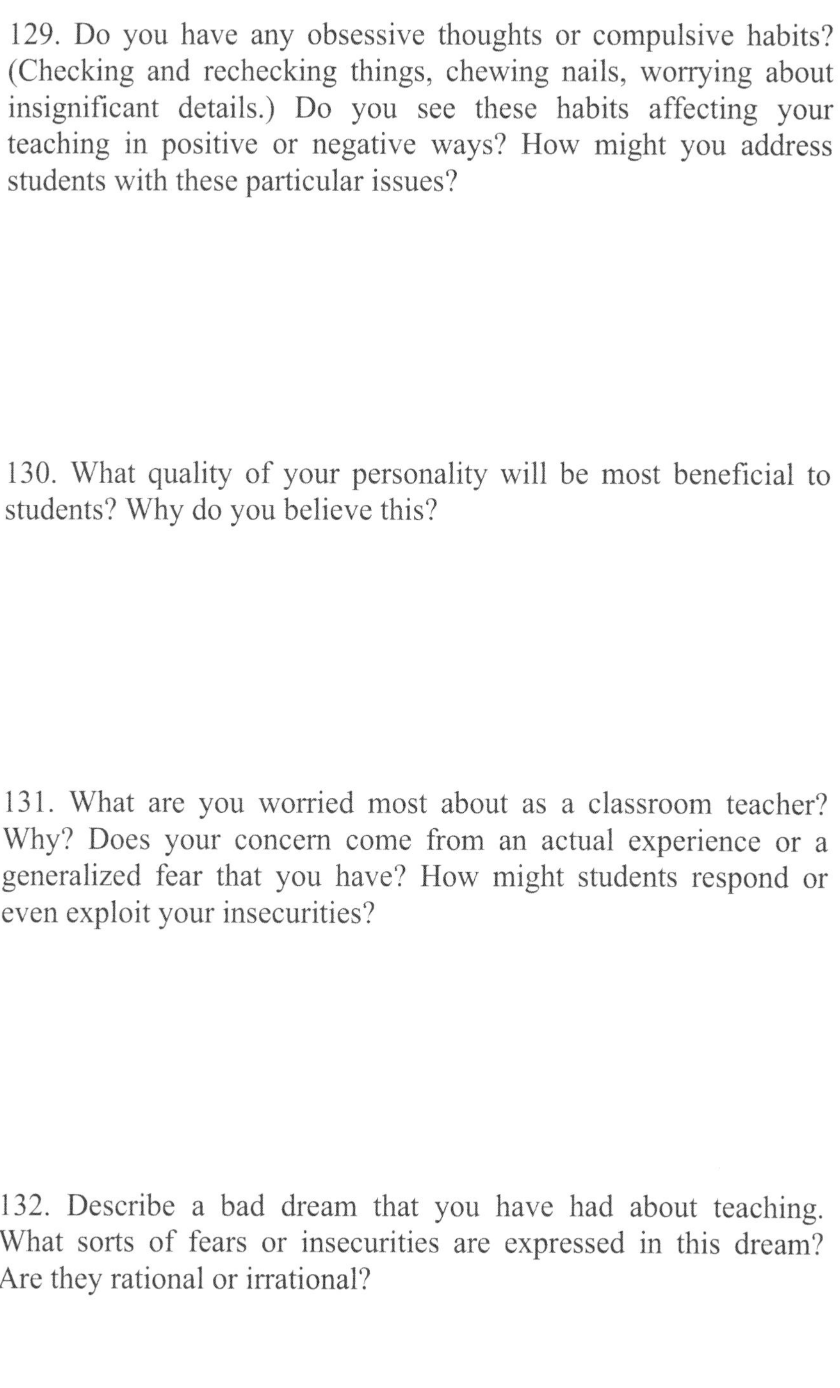

129. Do you have any obsessive thoughts or compulsive habits? (Checking and rechecking things, chewing nails, worrying about insignificant details.) Do you see these habits affecting your teaching in positive or negative ways? How might you address students with these particular issues?

130. What quality of your personality will be most beneficial to students? Why do you believe this?

131. What are you worried most about as a classroom teacher? Why? Does your concern come from an actual experience or a generalized fear that you have? How might students respond or even exploit your insecurities?

132. Describe a bad dream that you have had about teaching. What sorts of fears or insecurities are expressed in this dream? Are they rational or irrational?

133. How do you feel about crying in front of your students?

134. Under what circumstances would you apologize to the class? A student? A parent? Your boss? Would you do it in person, by phone, e-mail or some other way?

135. Under what circumstances would you expect an apology from a student? A parent? A class? Your boss?

136. Will your in-classroom personality be the same as your out-of-classroom personality? What are the advantages and disadvantages of any crossover between these two aspects of your personality?

Before and After School

137. Do you anticipate taking work home or getting everything done at school?

138. If school starts at 8am, what time would you arrive on an average day? What's the earliest that you would be willing to arrive? Would you set up office hours for students to come see you?

139. If school ends at 3pm, what time will you typically plan to leave? What's the latest that you would be willing to stay?

140. Would you help your students during prep periods? What about during your lunch?

141. How are you going to take care of your physical and mental health while you teach, especially the first few years? How often do you go to the doctor? Do you exercise regularly? Do you have a healthy diet? Would you ever consider therapy or psychiatric care? How do you plan on finding a balance between all of your needs and activities?

142. Would you ever take off of work when you weren't sick? What would warrant a day off for you? Do you believe that the idea of a mental health day off is valid? Do you believe that you are entitled to use all of your official sick days even if you are not actually sick?

143. When will recreation or other voluntary activities take precedence over work? What type of family responsibilities might cause you to miss work?

144. Would you spend time with colleagues outside of work? Boys: would you attend an outing for men only with teachers from your school? Girls: would you attend a girls' night with other female teachers from your school? How about mixed gender social activities?

145. Would you date another teacher from your school? How about an administrator?

146. What role will your significant other play in your teaching career? Do you think you'll have a long-term relationship with another teacher? If so, is it important that he or she approach teaching in a similar way? If not, how important is it to you that he or she understands your daily responsibilities?

147. Would you coach a sport or run another type of activity? What if the activity/club didn't personally interest you? Would you teach summer school?

148. Would you live in the community where you teach? Why or why not?

Personal Philosophy

149. Which movies about teachers/teaching have you seen? Do you think they are realistic? How are teachers portrayed? What can you learn from them?

150. If you had to write your own teacher movie, what would the plot be? What actor would you like to star in this movie?

151. Do you plan on keeping a journal of your teaching experiences? Why or why not? If so, what do you think you would write in it? Would you show it to anyone else? If so, whom?

152. How is teaching like or unlike: Coaching? Parenting? Babysitting? Dating? Judo? War? Musical conducting? Performing on stage? What is a good metaphor for teaching? What is a bad metaphor?

153. What will be your tone of voice when you are teaching the class as a whole? When you're trying to get their attention? When you "mean business"? When you're talking one-on-one with a student?

154. How comfortable would you be explaining what you know about RTI? PBIS? Common Core? National Boards? IEPs? 504 plans? Differentiation? Inquiry-based learning? What do you need to learn about these concepts, procedures and entities?

155. Is it ever appropriate to lower academic expectations for an entire class (from the official school expectations for that class or your own expectations)? Would you consider it appropriate to make an adjustment of the general expectations for a particular student if he or she did not have an IEP?

156. Are there any circumstances in which you would say you have done as much as possible for a class or an individual student and that she has to proceed on her own even if that might lead to some degree of failure?

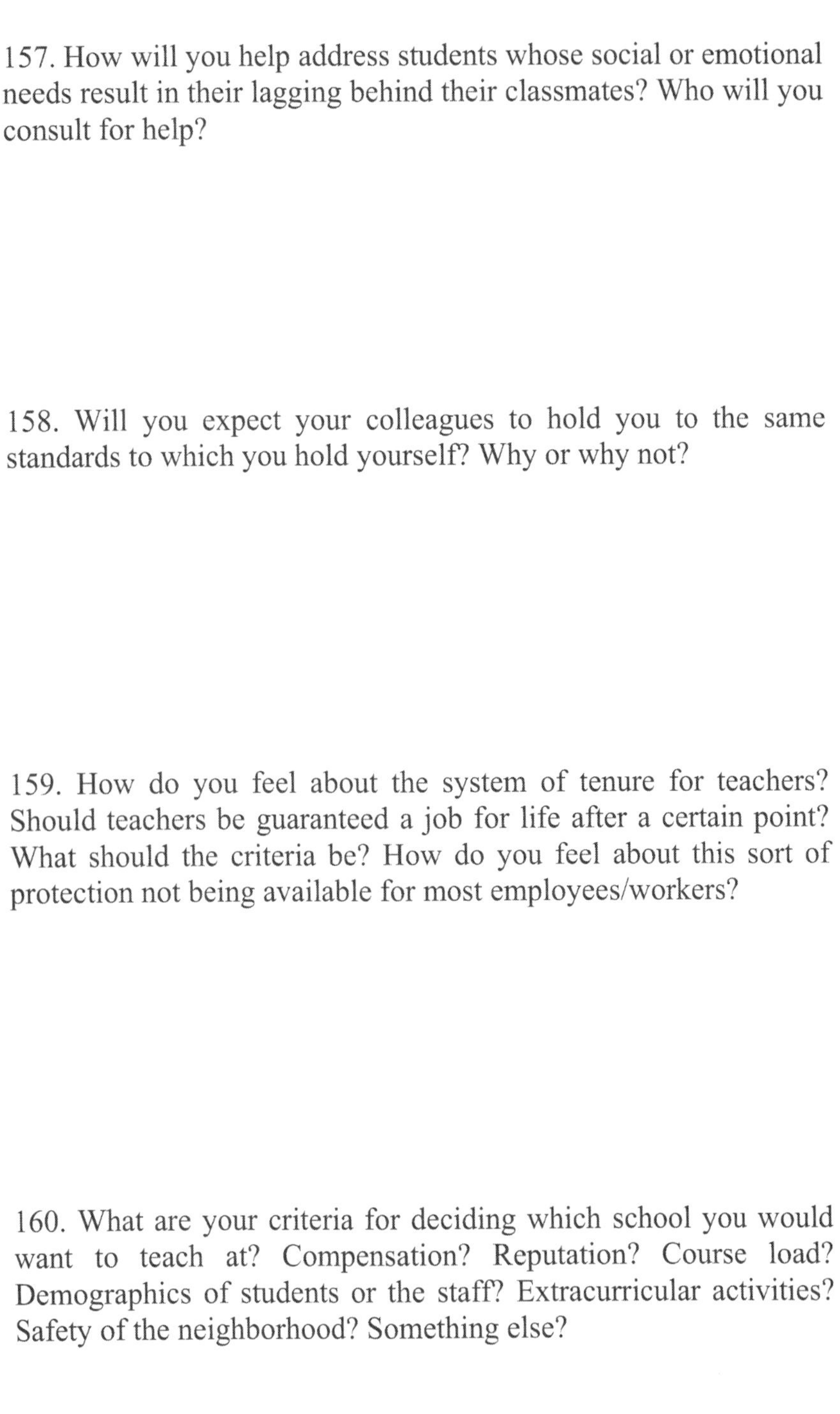

157. How will you help address students whose social or emotional needs result in their lagging behind their classmates? Who will you consult for help?

158. Will you expect your colleagues to hold you to the same standards to which you hold yourself? Why or why not?

159. How do you feel about the system of tenure for teachers? Should teachers be guaranteed a job for life after a certain point? What should the criteria be? How do you feel about this sort of protection not being available for most employees/workers?

160. What are your criteria for deciding which school you would want to teach at? Compensation? Reputation? Course load? Demographics of students or the staff? Extracurricular activities? Safety of the neighborhood? Something else?

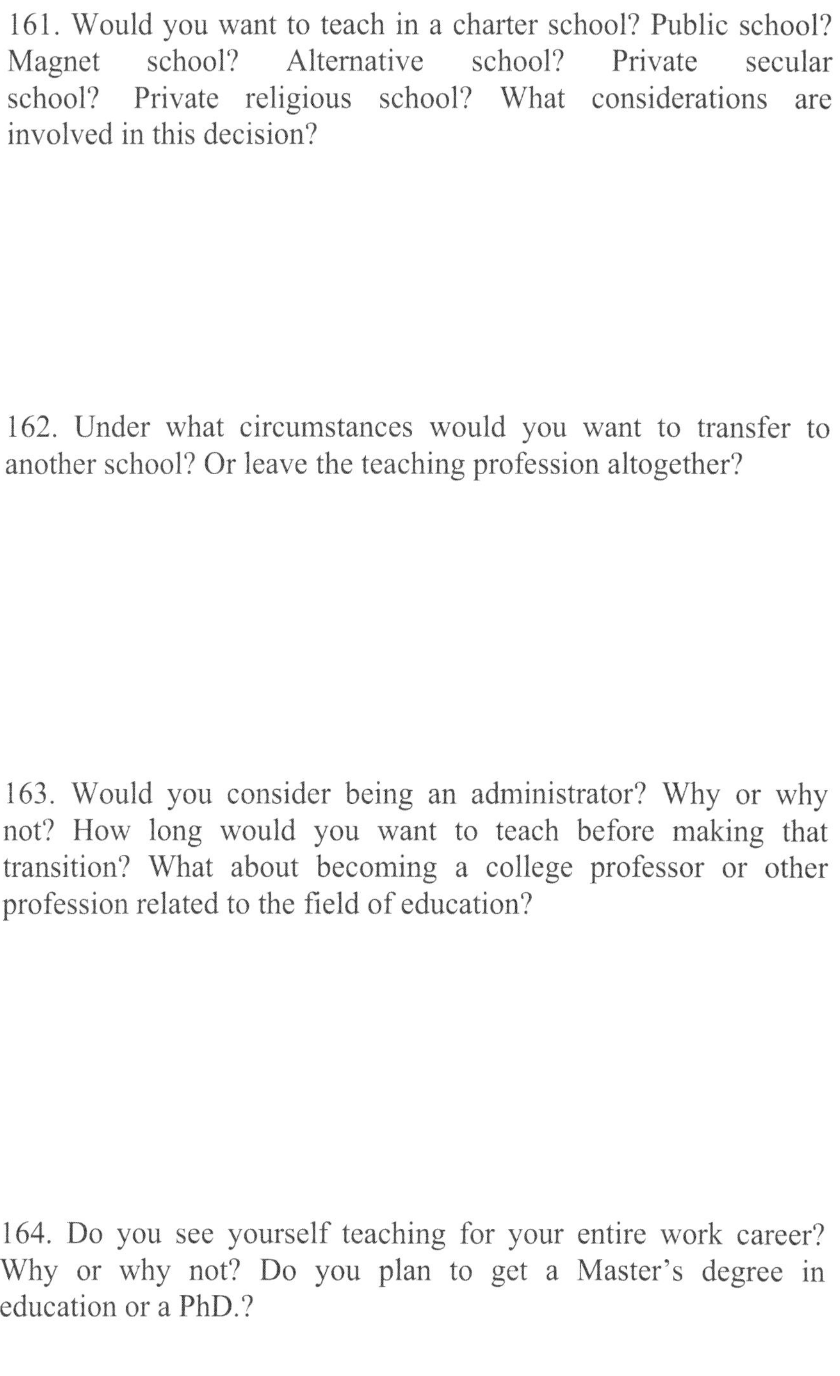

161. Would you want to teach in a charter school? Public school? Magnet school? Alternative school? Private secular school? Private religious school? What considerations are involved in this decision?

162. Under what circumstances would you want to transfer to another school? Or leave the teaching profession altogether?

163. Would you consider being an administrator? Why or why not? How long would you want to teach before making that transition? What about becoming a college professor or other profession related to the field of education?

164. Do you see yourself teaching for your entire work career? Why or why not? Do you plan to get a Master's degree in education or a PhD.?

Class Policy and Plans

165. What's your general plan for what you're going to do on your first day of classes? How will you introduce yourself to your students? How will you structure their introductions to you and each other? What do you think are the most important things to know about each other initially?

166. When does a student deserve a second chance? For example, would you let students retake tests? Under what conditions would you allow that?

167. Did you ever cheat on a test in school? Copy homework? How will you react if you see students engaging in either of these activities? Since cheating includes plagiarism (which may be difficult to detect), how do you plan to address this problem, and how important is it to you?

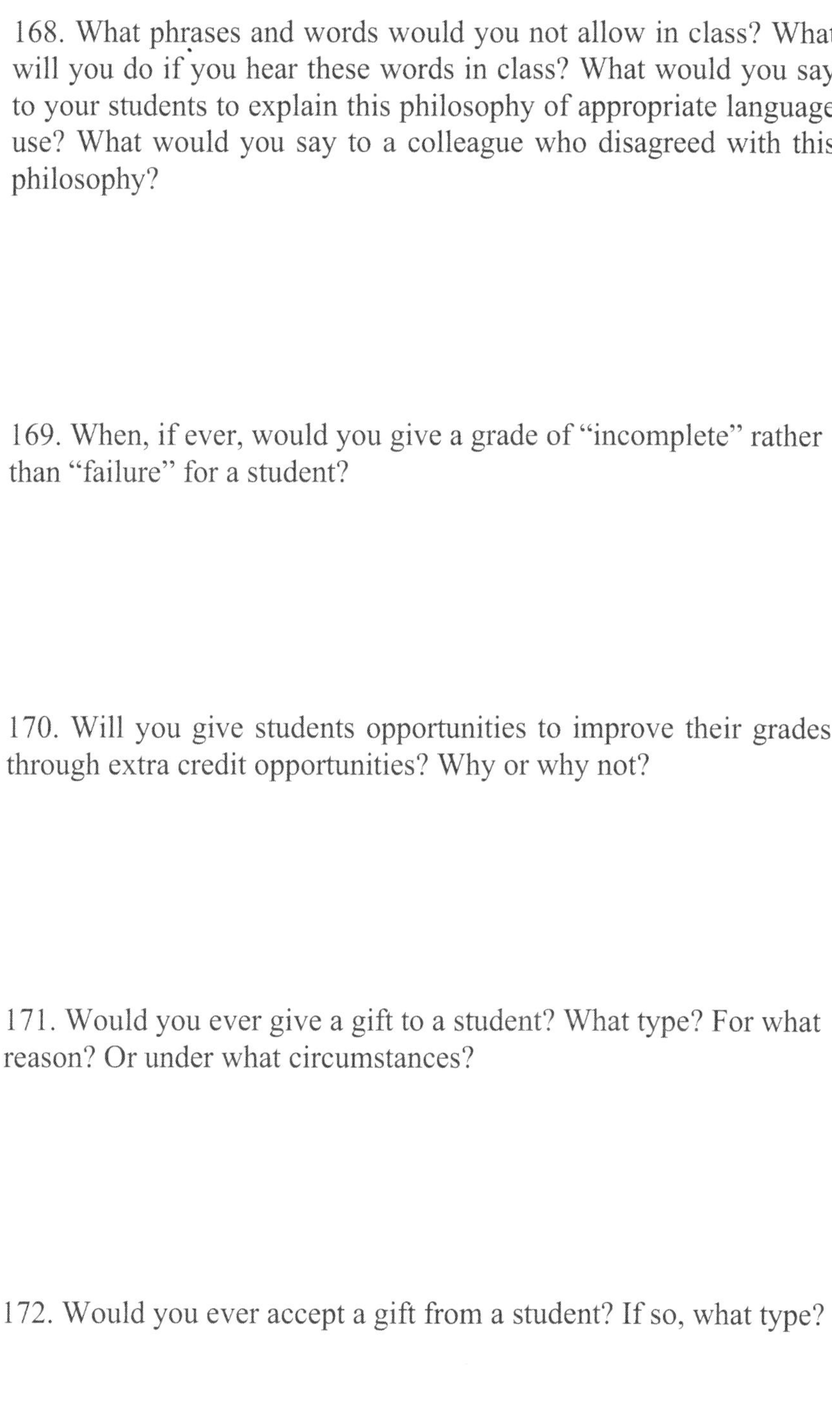

168. What phrases and words would you not allow in class? What will you do if you hear these words in class? What would you say to your students to explain this philosophy of appropriate language use? What would you say to a colleague who disagreed with this philosophy?

169. When, if ever, would you give a grade of "incomplete" rather than "failure" for a student?

170. Will you give students opportunities to improve their grades through extra credit opportunities? Why or why not?

171. Would you ever give a gift to a student? What type? For what reason? Or under what circumstances?

172. Would you ever accept a gift from a student? If so, what type?

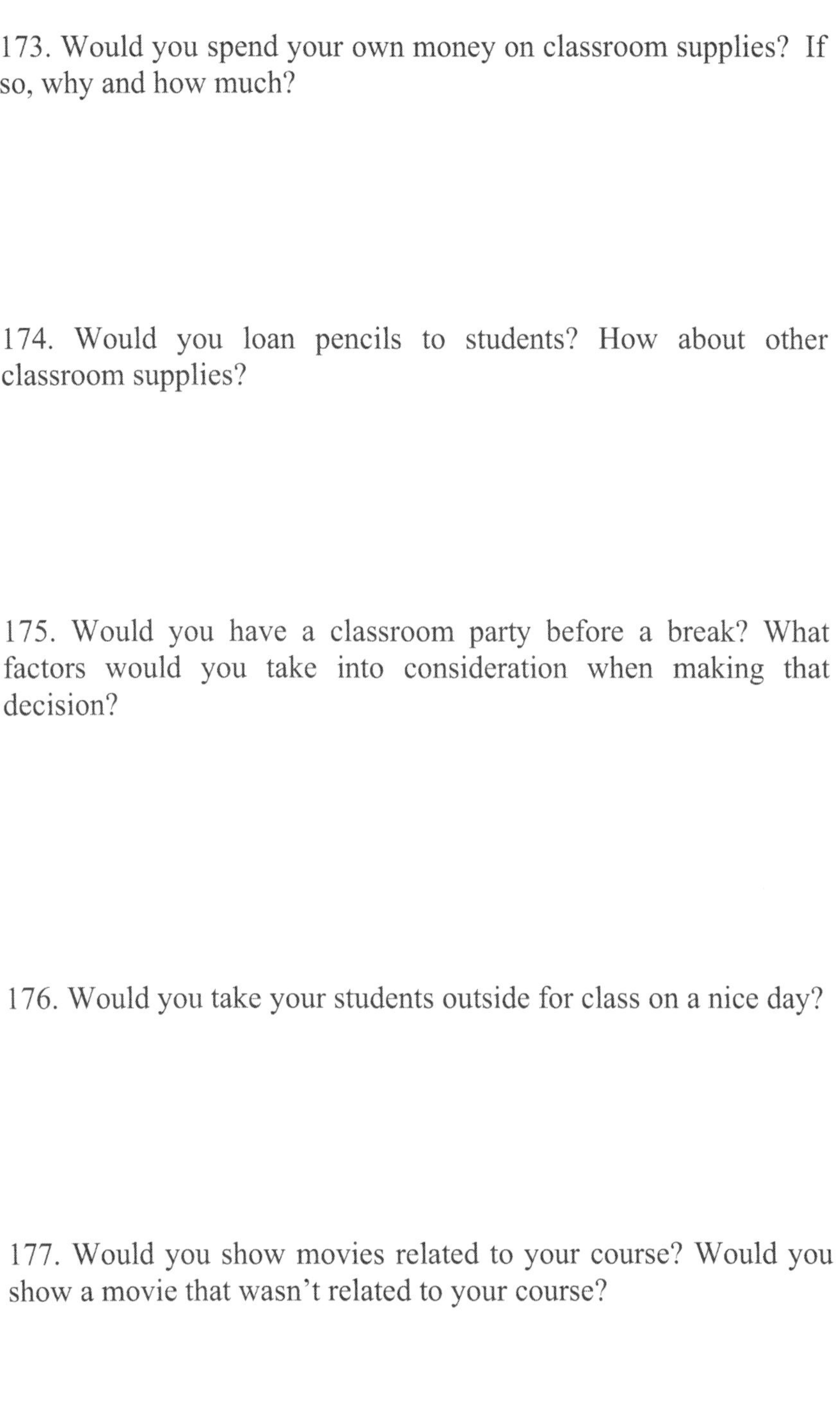

173. Would you spend your own money on classroom supplies? If so, why and how much?

174. Would you loan pencils to students? How about other classroom supplies?

175. Would you have a classroom party before a break? What factors would you take into consideration when making that decision?

176. Would you take your students outside for class on a nice day?

177. Would you show movies related to your course? Would you show a movie that wasn't related to your course?

178. Would you ever have a class pet (animal)? What factors go into that decision?

179. Will you have a "teacher stash" (Granola bars, toothbrush, etc.)? If so, what will you put in it?

180. Would you give your students food or medicine (cough drops, Advil, etc.)?

181. Would you let your students use your classroom phone? Classroom computer? Cell phone? Personal computer?

182. Would you give a student a ride in your car? Would you accept a ride in a student's car?

Chapter 2

Relationships With Students

Whether I was teaching honors students or struggling learners, I learned quickly that surviving a day of school was less dependent on the lesson plans I created and more dependent on my ability to manage the various personalities in a given classroom. Often it felt like my class was a slot machine with twenty five reels spinning at different rates. Sometimes they lined up for a jackpot of a lesson, but most of the time they were misaligned with no payoff.

In fact, for the most challenging classes, *I could never predict* the students' various states of mind before they crossed the threshold of my classroom. Together they might be a boiling pot of anger or a cold gazpacho soup, neither of which I particularly favored. Individually, they could be different in ways that I was only beginning to understand as a first-year teacher, and my third period physics class typified this odd phenomenon.

In that very special class, I had two seemingly opposite students: Jasmine and Henry. Jasmine was 16 going on 25. She flaunted every part of herself, which often resulted in my own discomfort but never hers. She could focus in class as long as her personal life wasn't interfering (and it usually was). Henry was your classic case of a student who was bullied for being different, except that he had a secret weapon; he made vulgar passes at his oppressors. He wore his trademark cashmere scarf as both a statement of style and an animalistic warning display. On multiple occasions, I watched him eviscerate bullies with sarcastic comments like, "Oh, I'd love to have a few minutes alone with you." I distinctly remember being tongue-tied by Jasmine and Henry two weeks before the end of the school year.

Jasmine marches in after the bell rings, and the volume of her clacking heels tells me that I have a problem on my hands. All hopes of ignoring it fade when she bitterly complains to the class about being denied the right to bring her over-21-year-old boyfriend to prom. A chorus of advice rains down on her, and the class no longer belongs to me.

I could try the old standby of, "Listen up class" or "Eyes on me," but I decide I need something with more punch so I quip, "Well, Jasmine, maybe you should stop dating older men."

Henry doesn't miss a beat before he announces to the class, "That's why I stopped dating older men."

I am flustered by such flagrant homosexual bravado and can only manage to blush and giggle.

"I don't know what to say," I finally get out.

"Just say 'yes' Mr. Podolner, just say 'YES!'" Henry bellows.

At this point, I had lost all composure. It was one thing to manage the comments of a sexually precocious teenage girl, but being the recipient of lascivious remarks from a teenage boy was more than I was trained to handle.

I truly don't remember how I extricated myself from that situation, but it wasn't the first or last time that I became a speechless teacher. Luckily, I had already developed strong relationships with both Henry and Jasmine, an investment that continued to pay dividends, particularly when I was at a loss for either words or actions. Sometimes, just saying or not saying anything made a huge difference with the kids I knew well. I realized early on that I had the ability to make a large negative or positive impact on them with a simple comment, facial expression or even an omission. Despite this personalized approach, there were also students whom I struggled to reach all year without success. They are the ones that linger in my mind as June turns into July. I wonder if I could have done something differently to break through to them.

Since teachers can maintain both effective and ineffective relationships with students, the way we interact with all of our students is critical. Teacher-student relations are incredibly complex with substantial room for both stunning success and abject failure. Most modern writing on education emphasizes the importance of strong student-teacher relationships, particularly for students who aren't doing well in school. The difficult aspect of this approach is that a successful student-teacher relationship means that the teacher has to play many conflicting roles simultaneously. For example with Jasmine, the paternal side of me wanted to put the brakes on her fast-forwarded sexuality while my legal status as a mandated reporter made me wonder if I had to tell somebody about her relationship with an adult. At the same time, it seemed that my primary job was to teach her physics and all else should have been secondary. However, to be able to teach her anything, I first had to gain her trust and respect, which meant acting more like a supportive counselor and sometimes just a friendly adult.

Determining the right approach with Henry was even more difficult. At the time, I didn't know if he was actually gay, or if his persona was something he created to make people feel uncomfortable. If he was indeed homosexual, it was important that he knew that my classroom was a safe zone for students of all sexual orientations, but if he feigned homosexuality as a tool to get what he wanted, that was cause for concern. Being on the receiving end of his comments put me in an uneasy position. My own teaching style was to use humor and comfortable student-teacher interactions to create a productive learning environment, though I ran the risk of students not always knowing the line between what was appropriate class commentary and what wasn't. Additionally, if he was gay, I didn't know if he was actually making some sexual advance towards me or just engaging in a public joke.

After more one-on-one conversations with Henry, I learned that he was gay but was not personally interested in me. As the year went on, I was able to draw him more towards appropriate behavior by accepting him for who he was and not overreacting when he was out of line. The point is that so many non-academic interactions between teachers and students have the potential for causing problems, but they are also opportunities for the engagement that leads towards deeper learning on various levels. Teachers must develop a sense of what is acceptable in their own classrooms but stay mindful of the dynamics of each class of students.

Relationships with Students

201. What do you expect your students will know about the subject matter of your class when they enter your classroom? What misconceptions about your subject do you expect them to have?

202. Do you believe that students need to be taught how to study? Do you know how to teach students how to study given the variety of learning styles they may have? How would you teach this process?

203. How will you greet your students each day (or period)? Explain the reason for your choice.

¤ At the door
¤ Individually after they enter
¤ As a whole class

204. In general, how are you going to get students' attention when you want to begin something or transition to a new topic? What will you do if you need to get them back on track?

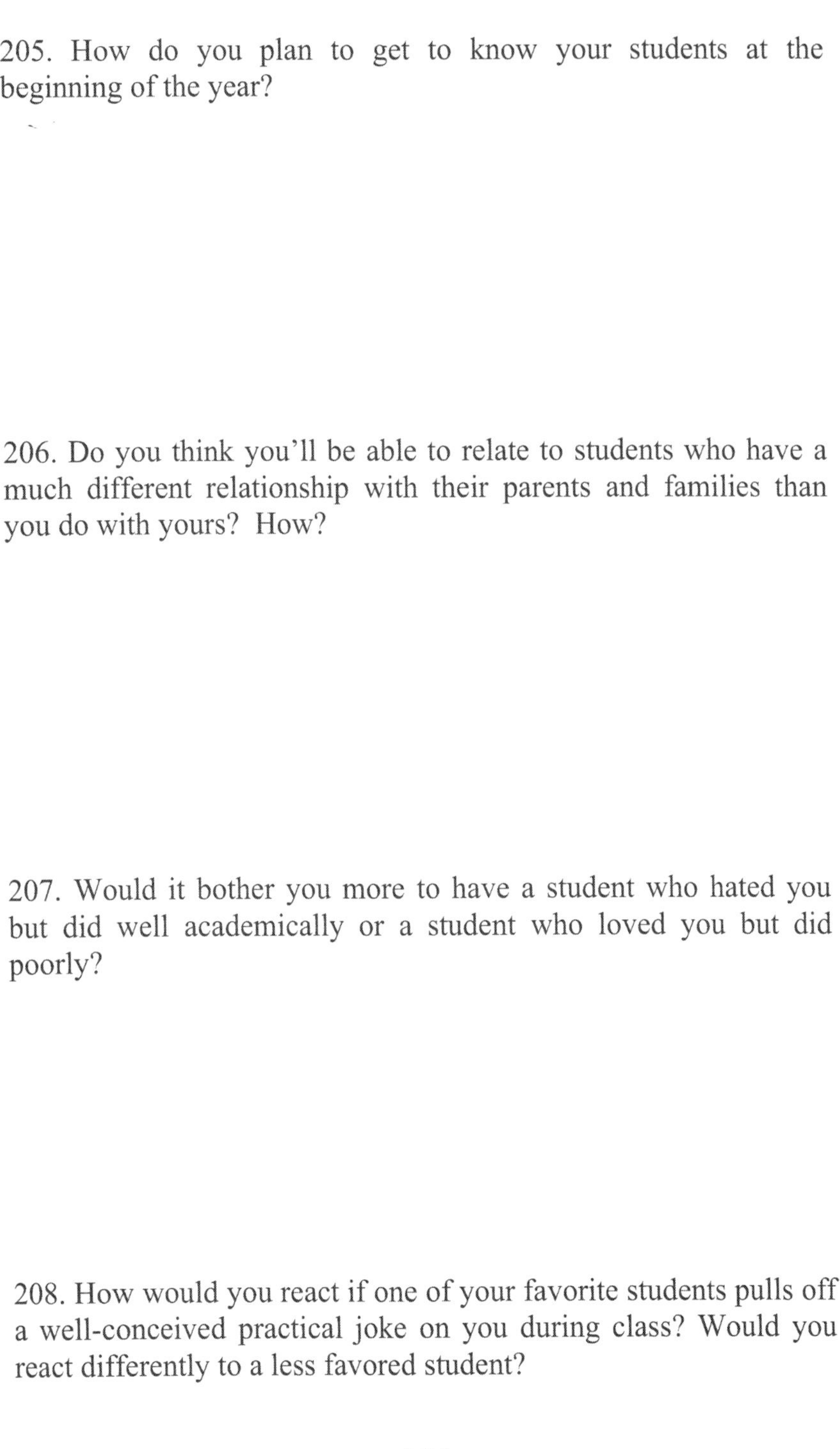

205. How do you plan to get to know your students at the beginning of the year?

206. Do you think you'll be able to relate to students who have a much different relationship with their parents and families than you do with yours? How?

207. Would it bother you more to have a student who hated you but did well academically or a student who loved you but did poorly?

208. How would you react if one of your favorite students pulls off a well-conceived practical joke on you during class? Would you react differently to a less favored student?

209. Do you see yourself having a teacher's pet? Would it bother you if your students thought you had favorites?

210. What student behaviors would you tolerate while you teach? Explain your choices.

¤ Tapping on the desk
¤ Having a quiet conversation with a neighbor
¤ Reading a book other than the text
¤ Doing homework for another class
¤ Brushing hair
¤ Texting
¤ Listening to an iPod or other device
¤ Putting on lotion
¤ Putting on makeup
¤ Singing
¤ Doodling

What "stories" come to mind when you observe these behaviors? Let's say a student is doodling – does that mean he is bored or disinterested in the subject? If a girl is putting on makeup, what does that tell you about her priorities?

211. What student behaviors would you tolerate when they are working in groups?

¤ Talking about non-school related activities
¤ Braiding each other's hair
¤ Putting lotion on each other
¤ Talking to other groups
¤ Listening to their iPods

How would you respond when a student or students engage in these activities? What if they continue to do it after you tell them to stop?

212. What can you share about yourself without revealing information that is too personal? What areas of self-disclosure are taboos?

213. Would you ever let your students call you something besides Mr. or Ms./Mrs.? How about a nickname? Your first name?

214. How would you feel if you heard a student describing you as his friend? What if he described you as "not like other teachers"?

215. Would you be Facebook friends with your students? Twitter? Instagram? Any other social media? If your answer is "yes," what parameters would you put on your postings and what postings would you allow from the students and former students? What about your colleagues? Your administrators? If your answer is "no," what are the reasons for precluding this option?

216. Would you buy anything from a student, such as for a fundraiser? Would you sell anything to your students, like school supplies? Would you ask one of your students or former students to fix your personal computer, for example, or provide another service to you, either for free or for a fee?

217. Would you give money to a student? Under what circumstances?

218. What could students do that would put you in a better mood?

219. How are you going to find a balance between humor and seriousness in class? Do you think you might be more inclined to be overly-serious or the opposite? Would you try too hard to joke around at the students' level?

220. What is your comfort level for physical touch with students? Would fears of administrative or legal action against you restrict your inclination to provide supportive touch? Do you think you would respond differently regarding physical touch depending on the gender or sexual orientation of the student?

221. Would you do something to foster a relationship between two of your students in one of your classes? For example, would you seat two students next to each other who might be romantically interested in each other? Or would you discourage romantic inclinations between students by seating them apart? Also, might you pair two students together who are both in need of a good friend?

222. How would you feel about two students holding hands in class? Hugging? Sitting on laps? Massaging each other? Kissing? Would your answers be different if the couple was LGBT?

223. Would you write a job or college recommendation for a student who didn't impress you? If not, what would you say to the student when you refused him? If yes, would you exaggerate his qualifications?

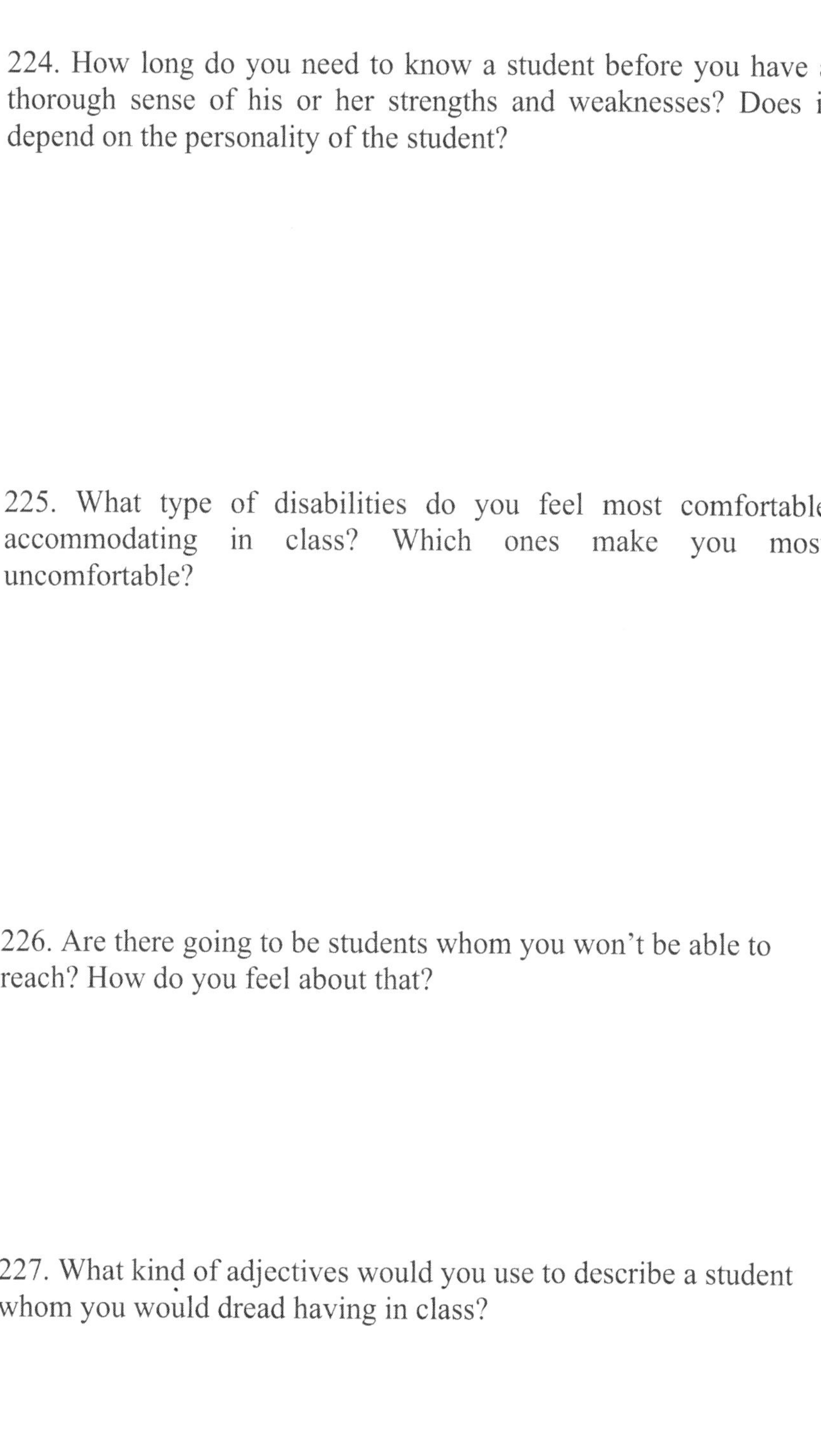

224. How long do you need to know a student before you have a thorough sense of his or her strengths and weaknesses? Does it depend on the personality of the student?

225. What type of disabilities do you feel most comfortable accommodating in class? Which ones make you most uncomfortable?

226. Are there going to be students whom you won't be able to reach? How do you feel about that?

227. What kind of adjectives would you use to describe a student whom you would dread having in class?

228. What kind of adjectives would you use to describe your ideal student?

229. What information would you want to know about your students on a daily or weekly basis? Explain your choices.

¤ Recent fight with parents/friends
¤ Sexual activity
¤ New boyfriend/girlfriend
¤ Use of illicit substances
¤ Grades in other classes
¤ Success in school endeavors
¤ Success in outside of school endeavors
¤ General emotional state
¤ Sleeping habits
¤ Break up with boyfriend/girlfriend
¤ Other

What will you do when students start to share information that you don't want to know?

230. What sort of student behavior would you consider threatening?

231. What might a student do or say to make you think he or she is a victim of physical, sexual or emotional abuse?

232. What sort of signs would you look for to tell if a student is suffering from mental health issues?

233. Do you think it's possible that you could hate a student? What might he do to cause such a reaction in you?

234. What could a student do outside of school that would enhance your opinion of her? What could a student do outside of school that would lower your opinion of her? Of the actions that lower your opinion, what could you forgive or accept? What action could irreparably damage your acceptance of a student, or your capacity to interact positively with him in a professional manner?

235. How do you accept students for who they are as students while simultaneously encouraging them to move in the direction you want them to go? Is this a contradiction or a resolvable paradox?

236. How are your students going to evaluate you? Through some formal survey, or another way? How do you think you will respond if they rate some aspect of your teaching very negatively? What if that aspect was intrinsic to either your personality or the course you teach?

237. Are there students who talk, look or dress "smarter" than others? Is it possible for you to overcome these negative stereotypes about how students present themselves? How will you do this?

238. Do you want your students to respect you? Like you? Fear you? Love you? What are the repercussions of seeking approval and/or adoration from your students?

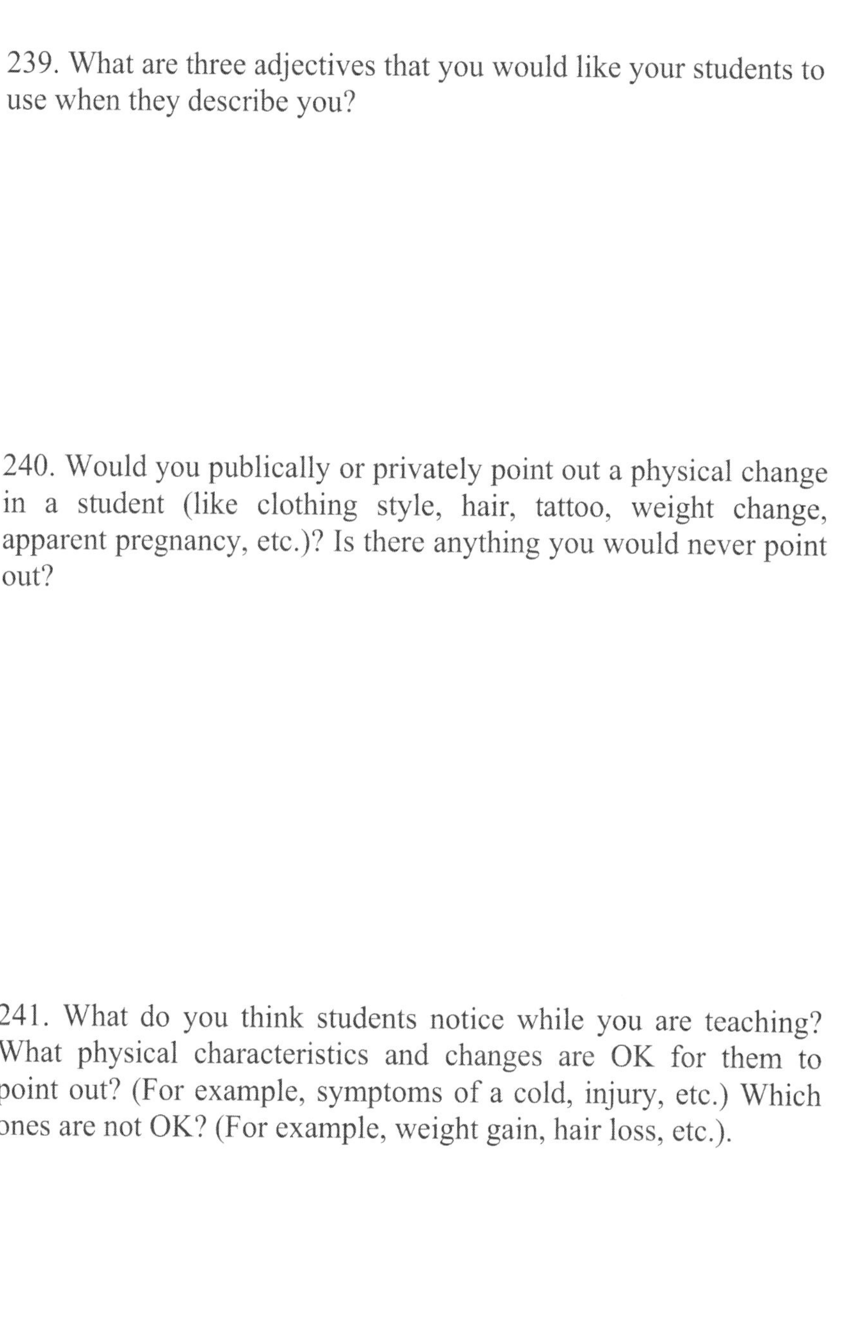

239. What are three adjectives that you would like your students to use when they describe you?

240. Would you publically or privately point out a physical change in a student (like clothing style, hair, tattoo, weight change, apparent pregnancy, etc.)? Is there anything you would never point out?

241. What do you think students notice while you are teaching? What physical characteristics and changes are OK for them to point out? (For example, symptoms of a cold, injury, etc.) Which ones are not OK? (For example, weight gain, hair loss, etc.).

242. Can you control your facial expressions such that you can communicate disapproval of misbehavior with a certain "look"? Can you show approval non-verbally? Will your students be able to read your expressions?

243. How do you think you would react if you found out a student posted about you on a social media website? Would it matter if it was positive or negative? What if it included a picture of you that he took without permission?

Chapter 3

Relationships With Parents

As a recent alumnus of the high school where I am employed, my first relationships with parents and students were far from normal. Among my students were kids I babysat, my younger sister's friends and the siblings of my peers. I mostly relished the sense of familiarity that came with teaching at my hometown school, but there were pitfalls too. For example, I shouldn't have been surprised when a parent answered the phone asking, "Is this the same Aaron Podolner that took my daughter to homecoming?" Even worse was when one of my students decided that the middle of class would be a good time to give me the belt I left at her sister's house.

Besides the embarrassment of having my personal life aired in public, there were stressful interactions with parents as well. A neighbor of my parents tried to bend the prerequisite rules to get her son into my class, and another dad worked hard to make sure I gave his daughter special treatment. Other parents tried to take advantage of my status as a new teacher who had a long-standing relationship with their children to extract concessions on grades. One mom even called my mom to demand that I move a test back a day.

The mixture of courses I taught during that first year was both impossible and perfect. I started with a co-taught special education math course, ran off to the science wing for two sections of honors physics, flew upstairs for remedial math and looped back around near my starting point for honors geometry. Though I mastered the logistics, the task was impossible because I felt too young and inexperienced to meet the needs of my wide range of students. It was also perfect because I gained a broad perspective on the types of students and parents I would work with for years to come. I worked with parents who demanded to know how to raise their daughter's A- to an A, and I tried to counsel students whose parents were in and out of jail. I did my best, but I know now that every interaction could have gone better. In that way, the students of first-year teachers are the sacrificial lambs for those who follow them; their peers to come gain what they lose themselves.

It doesn't have to be that way. First-year teachers can be better, and a significant part has to do with the way they involve parents in the education of their students. This can be a difficult task because parent/teacher relationships are probably the area most fraught with ambiguity. School policy on the issue tends to be limited. At my school, for example, we are encouraged to contact parents of students with Ds and Fs and only provide documentation of conversations and interventions if the student ends up failing the course. Our union urges us to call the parents of struggling students, but probably would be less enthusiastic if a teacher called parents at night from her cell phone or spent the weekend responding to parent e-mails because that goes far beyond our contractual duties. A simple rule could be that teachers and parents should work together on what's best for the student, but "what's best" is debatable. Some parents make this process more difficult because they confuse advocating for their child with advocating for their child's grade.

Every year I have at least a handful of students who have major problems writing down assignments, doing their homework, and then turning it in the next day. As I troubleshoot ways to improve their grades with parents, I am often asked:

Can you check his assignment notebook daily before he leaves?

Can you ask for her homework at the beginning of class?
Can you email me every time he fails to turn in an assignment?
Can you send a weekly agenda on Monday?

These requests are in addition to the website I maintain with all of the assignments and the online grade book available to parents. While I know that complying will possibly improve the grades of these students, I'm not sure these actions are ultimately helpful for the student's sense of responsibility for his or her own education. This uncertainty creates one of the most difficult tensions I encounter as a teacher:

> To what extent do I treat my students like children who need nurturing, support and forgiveness, and to what extent do I treat my students like young adults who need to experience the natural consequences of their actions?

Further complicating this tension is the presence of students with various learning, emotional and behavioral disabilities. Students with known disabilities in public schools may have Individualized Education Plans (IEPs). These plans are mandated by the Individuals with Disabilities Education Act (IDEA) and spell out the educational objectives for a student along with accommodations for anything from scheduling adjustments to the use of a one-on-one aide. Common accommodations are extended time on tests, no penalty for in class spelling errors and an assigned note taker for the student. The IEPs also describe the student's specific disability and a summary of testing done to establish the diagnosis.

One of my goals for this book is to convince you to be as honest as possible about every aspect of yourself, your teaching and the way you interact with all types of students. In order to share an experience that taught me a tremendous lesson, I will frankly admit the one disability that makes me most anxious: Asperger's Syndrome, an Autism Spectrum Disorder. Although it is not included separately in the DSMV (Diagnostic and Statistical Manual for Mental Disorders, version five), the main characteristics are generally clear: difficulty with social interactions, a rigid thought process and eccentric self-soothing behaviors. In lecture-based class with no group work, I think my first student with autism, David, would have been able to function without difficulty. Instead, and like many modern classrooms, mine is more open and oriented towards group work. My students learn quickly when to be serious and when they can fool around. They figure out what jokes are appropriate and which ones are not. They transition easily from partner sharing to group work to whole class discussions. Because of his disability, David had difficulty with all of these transitions and adjustments.

To aggravate matters, I didn't know how to help him and found myself continually frustrated with his behavior. At the November conferences with his parents, I mentioned that he often came across as obnoxious. They didn't say much that evening, but the next day his mom sent me an e-mail indicating that they were perturbed by my comment and demanded a meeting with me and David's school-appointed case manager. Before the meeting the case manager mentioned something that I'll never forget: David was their baby.

Their baby, the one they brought into this world. The one they soothed when he was fussing. The one they puzzled over when he didn't behave like other little kids. And the one they still fight for today to make sure he gets the same opportunities as other students.

I kept that in mind during the meeting, and it went well. We talked about how to help David progress and tensions were resolved until after first semester exams -- a large part of his final grade was a project that David did incorrectly despite instructions and student examples. His parents were not pleased with this outcome and requested an additional accommodation at the annual review of David's IEP.

When I read the new accommodation, I was irate. It was something like, "David's teachers will personally explain large projects to him and ensure that he understands all expectations." This wasn't merely a suggestion, it was part of a legally binding document, and any failure to comply with it was grounds for a legal action. To me, this change in the IEP was a symptom of grade seeking at the expense of life lessons and misuse of the special education system to put unreasonable onus on the teacher. Moreover, it seemed like this change was a legal maneuver to imply that I didn't properly address David's disability. I felt that no teacher can guarantee that what he does will be absorbed by a student, especially if the educational goal is beyond the child's capacity. So I wrote an angry e-mail to the parents and copied it to the case manager.

Then I remembered that David was their most precious possession in the world, and I did not click "send." Instead, I called his mom and had a constructive conversation. I asked her calmly what they were looking for in the newest accommodation, and she explained. As it turns out, they weren't looking to create some sort of "gotcha" document; they only wanted to add to the tools for helping David, their baby. As the second half of the year unfolded, David did get a better sense of how to navigate my class socially, and I even learned to like his humor. I stopped forcing him to work with other students during labs and took extra time to ensure that he understood the 2nd semester project. He finished the year splendidly.

I'm still troubled when I have to decide between helping a student directly, or helping a student by insisting he figure something out on his own, though I am better now at partnering with parents and guardians, especially after having my own children. When my first child came into the world, I knew immediately that I would do *anything* to protect and support her. I try to remember that every time I call a student's home.

I should be clear that there are potentially challenging interactions with parents of regular education students, too. Once, a mom called me to complain about the grade on a final project. She was very angry, and it actually took a while for me to figure out what prompted her call. After listening carefully, I tried my best to reflect back what I thought was the crux of her argument: "So what I hear you saying is that just because Andre did the final project and turned something in, he should have received at least a D (for effort), instead of an F despite leaving out major portions of the assignment?" Even though I'm pretty sure that's exactly what she had been saying, she disagreed and went on to say that she was mad that I gave Andre an F because he is going to be an engineer. Then she promptly hung up on me.

I was miffed at the time, but over the years, I slowly figured out what could have been the subtext of our conversation from her perspective. I was a white man essentially saying that a young black man would not be able to fulfill his dreams. I don't know anything about that mom personally, but it is likely that she had experienced discrimination throughout her life and saw this grade as further evidence of a system that was stacked against her and her family. To this day, I am still more anxious when I call non-white parents. I don't overtly mention racism or privilege during these conversations, but it's always in the back of my mind.

This awareness of the experience that our students' families have with racism and discrimination certainly does not generally mean that we need to lower the standards for a passing grade on an assignment or an entire course. Were we to lower our expectations on the basis of race alone, we would be contributing to what is generally regarded as part of the problem of institutional racism -- expecting too little of students of color.

Understanding the role of race, culture and poverty in minority communities is critical to understanding the background of our students and the frustrations of their parents if their children do not succeed. The point of using your reflection on the backgrounds of your students is to help you to make up for some of the environmentally caused educational deficiencies that exist. Moreover, the more you understand what your students and their parents have experienced, the more likely you are to build a positive working relationship with all parties involved.

Relationships with Parents

301. What do you feel the role of parents/guardians is (or should be) regarding the classroom? Outside of the classroom? What can or should you do if a parent is non-compliant with your expectations?

302. Describe the ideal parent of your students, and describe one that you fear most.

303. Would you feel comfortable giving your thoughts if a parent asked you for your frank advice as to how to deal with their child at home? If not, to whom would you make a referral?

304. What type(s) of parents/guardians will annoy you? How will you deal with this parent/guardian?

305. What type of conversation would you dread having with a parent? What kind of conversation would you look forward to having?

306. What sort of parent would you deliberately not call? If a situation arose that would normally warrant a parent call, what would you do instead?

307. What are you going to say to a parent if she blames you for her child's failures and refuses to take responsibility? What if she says the problem is your lack of experience?

308. What type of interaction with a parent would prompt you to seek the advice or counsel of a colleague? Your boss? Your significant other?

309. Under what circumstances, if any, would you hang up on a parent during a conversation?

310. A parent calls you to say that he doesn't like the student who is sitting next to his child in class because he feels the student is a bad influence on his child. You explain to the parent that you sat them together for other reasons, but he still requests that you change the students' seats. Would you comply?

311. For a large project, students are allowed to work in groups. A parent calls to say that he doesn't like the student his child chose to work with and feels the pairing will be detrimental to the students' grade. You talk to the students and they still want to stay together. Would you overrule their decision?

312. A parent asked you to write a report on his student every week. Would you comply? What about every day?

313. What will you say if a parent asks you to communicate via email her child's assignments every day?

314. You have a student who is struggling to write down assignments and turn them in. That child's parent asks you to take responsibility for checking that student's assignment notebook every day and asking the student personally for the assignment the next day. Would you comply?

315. Under what circumstances are you going to call parents? Would you call for positive news, as well as negative news?

316. You have called a parent a few times to report misbehaviors in class. The parent asks you to call her the next time it happens in class and put her on the phone so that she can discipline the student. Would you comply? If you wouldn't comply, how would you respond to the parent?

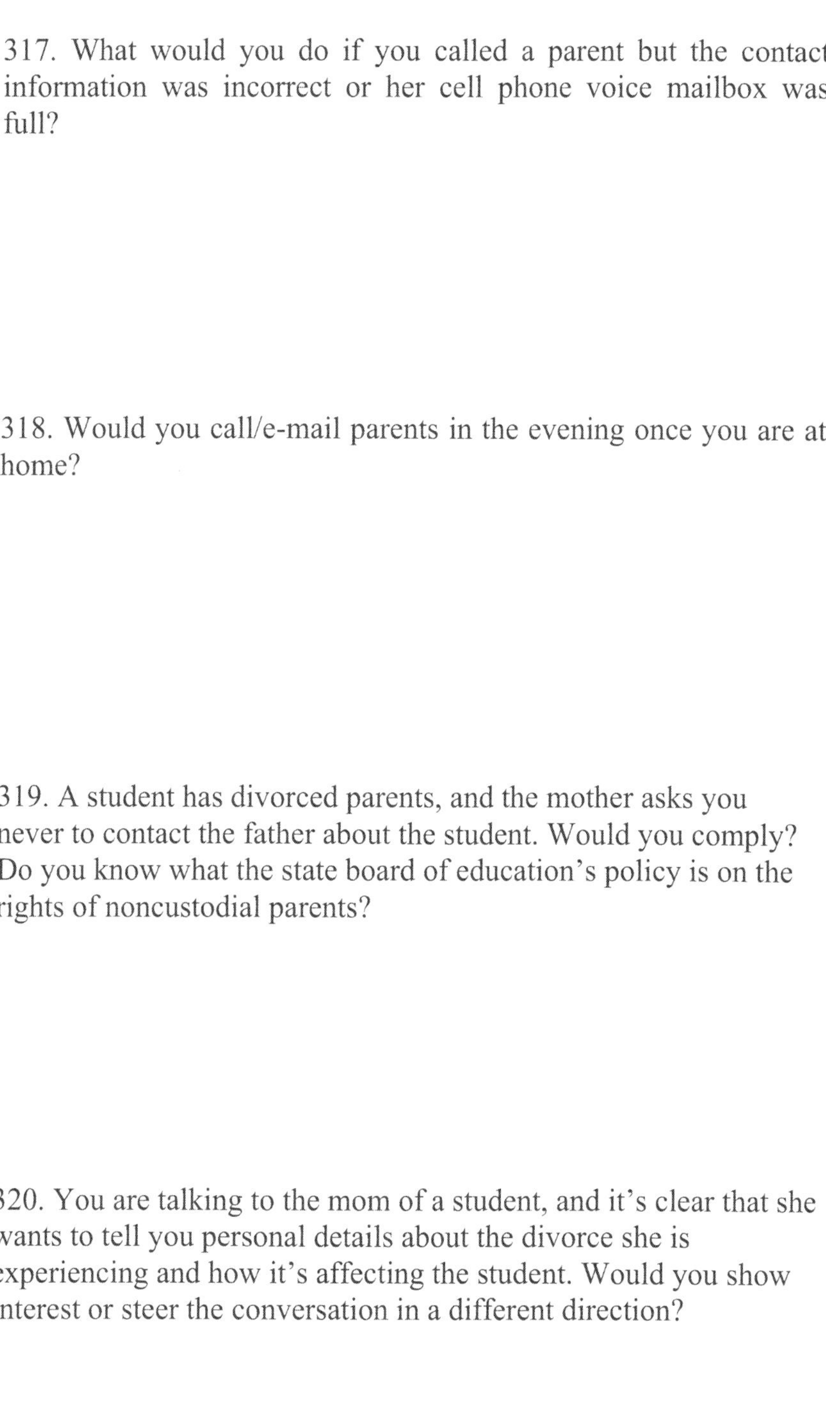

317. What would you do if you called a parent but the contact information was incorrect or her cell phone voice mailbox was full?

318. Would you call/e-mail parents in the evening once you are at home?

319. A student has divorced parents, and the mother asks you never to contact the father about the student. Would you comply? Do you know what the state board of education's policy is on the rights of noncustodial parents?

320. You are talking to the mom of a student, and it's clear that she wants to tell you personal details about the divorce she is experiencing and how it's affecting the student. Would you show interest or steer the conversation in a different direction?

321. How do you think the parents of your students view teachers in general?

322. If you are currently a parent, how do you think your children's teachers view you? How do you think having or not having your own children affects the way you interact with your students' parents?

323. How comfortable do you feel talking to parents of other races and socioeconomic backgrounds?

324. What would you do if a parent you needed to contact did not speak English?

325. If a child has two parents/guardians listed with contact info, how would you decide which one to call first?

326. Would you talk to a parent differently than a guardian? Would you talk to a family friend (often listed on student data sheets) differently than you would talk to a parent?

327. At parent/teacher conferences, would you prefer to have the student present or not? What if the parent belittles the student in front of you?

328. To what extent should your teaching style match the parenting style that your students experience at home?

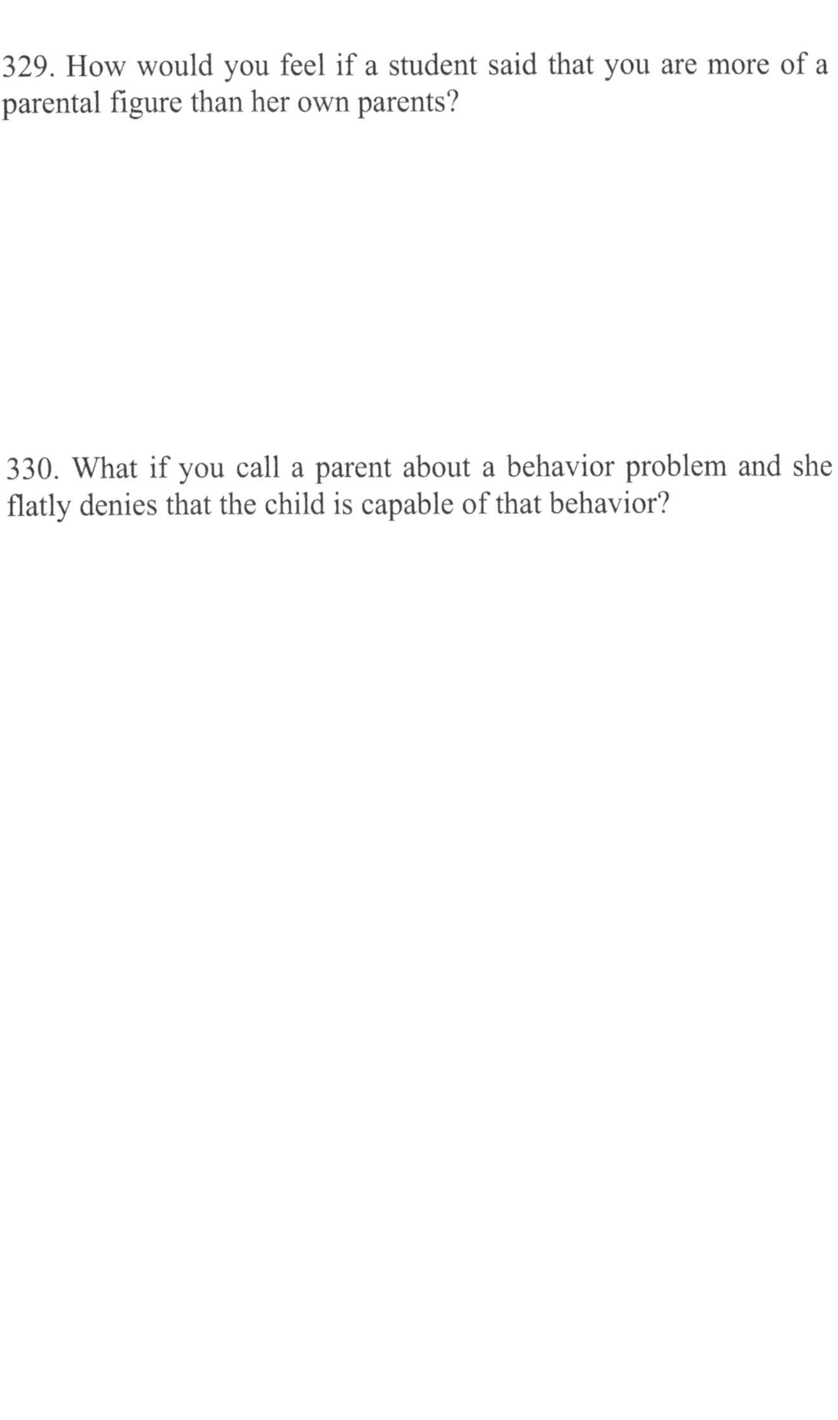

329. How would you feel if a student said that you are more of a parental figure than her own parents?

330. What if you call a parent about a behavior problem and she flatly denies that the child is capable of that behavior?

Chapter 4

Assumptions About Teaching

This is a difficult time to become a teacher.

Never has more been expected of teachers, and never have more politicians and other non-educators claimed to know what teachers should do. Being asked to do more than what's in a job description makes comparisons to other professions difficult. You wouldn't assume a plumber would put in overtime for free when a customer destroyed his pipes due to negligence. Nor would you expect lawyers to routinely work pro bono on the weekends for the greater good.

Obviously these analogies are imperfect – to outsiders there's almost no way to communicate how the teaching profession has been uniquely singled out to somehow solve societal problems that transcend the classroom, like poverty and broken families. Nonetheless, the role of a teacher has expanded from simply instructing and evaluating to include the following: teaching all types of learners, addressing students from all types of ethnic and cultural backgrounds, improving students' social/emotional skills, and generally making up for any deficits that students bring to class.

I am in *favor* of these expansions of teacher duties. It is a monumental responsibility to be a teacher -- we don't know when our job is done, and it is easy to convince ourselves that we should have done more. Even with the advent of research-based testing, it is nearly impossible to surmise the extent of our influence or truly understand the nature of our failures. Our successes are sometimes seen within the school year, but often we don't hear about the ways we have touched the lives of students over time. Despite the burden of this uncertainty, teachers should *still* do as much as they can for every student. However, as individual teachers, we cannot necessarily overcome the societal conditions that lead to poverty, discrimination, and lack of school funding.

What's difficult to tolerate is the barrage of uninformed voices in the most pressing educational issues today. This is worsened when so many modern educational solutions appear to be commonsensical. Once a position hardens into conventional wisdom, teachers struggle to show its flaws. For example:

**Of course* it is logical that you should test students to see what they are learning -- the more standardized and national the exam, the more we know about the effectiveness of teachers and schools.

*Competition between schools is a *no brainer* -- if economic competitiveness leads to superior products and increased efficiencies, the same should be true in education.

*It makes *complete sense* to have merit pay -- salesmen and managers get bonuses for doing well, and so should teachers.

As you can see, these are easy arguments to make, difficult to refute and have found wide acceptance outside of educational circles. A new teacher may think she can close the door and forget about these national movements and controversies, but individual educators are increasingly forced to take part in the debate.

In what seems to be an incongruous comparison, the changes in how teachers are viewed by the general public remind me of my journey from local school kid to temporary world traveler. In grades one through twelve, I was from Oak Park. When I went to college, I was from Chicago, but when I studied abroad in Madrid and traveled around Europe, I felt like an *American* for the first time because that's what people saw first when they met me. Suddenly, I was asked to defend everything from war in Iraq to capital punishment. I was totally unprepared to be an unofficial ambassador for my country.

Sadly, teachers are now treated as if they are travelling in a foreign and sometimes hostile country. They are asked by friends, family and strangers to defend their compensation, unions and pensions. They are treated by print, web and TV commentators as both scapegoats and saviors without any sense of irony. When I tell people that I teach, I still get lots of comments that indicate respect for the profession. Despite this general sense of admiration, I have been on the receiving end of more and more pointed comments and questions about policies related to education. Most of these arguments start with trite expressions like, "You know teachers only have to work from 8am to 3pm and get tons of time off" or, "teachers' unions protect lazy and ineffective teachers."

When I'm confronted by these often condescending, uninformed and stereotypical comments about teachers and schools, I first ask myself whether this person actually wants to have a conversation. Usually they do not. But some do, and their questions have forced me to do my own research on national, state, and local issues facing education. That's a good thing -- I spent the first ten years of my career just focusing on my students and while the recent public interest in education may be largely misplaced, it is nice to have an opportunity to explain what we do and how some of the so-called common knowledge about education has been distorted by political and private entities.

Assumptions about teaching -- do you agree or disagree? Explain your choice.

A community member might say:

401. Core classes should be taught in single-sex classrooms.

402. Students should wear identification badges in school.

403. Students should wear uniforms in school.

404. School lockers should be checked occasionally by drug-sniffing dogs.

405. Some people shouldn't be teachers.

406. Subject areas that are harder to fill (like science, math and special education) should pay higher than subjects that have a lot of candidates (like English, history and Physical Education).

407. Teachers who grade more papers (like History and English) should be paid more.

408. Teachers, in general, are paid too much.

409. Students aren't learning enough because the school year is too short.

410. Most of the problems in schools today are the result of taking God out of education.

A veteran teacher might say:

411. Giving extra credit opportunities is a good way to motivate students.

412. Most students will usually do the bare minimum to get the grade that they want.

413. Teachers should call on students during class discussions whether they want to be called on or not.

414. Teachers should assign students seats rather than students picking for themselves.

415. Class policies should be consistently enforced, regardless of a student's personal situation.

416. Teaching is part performance.

417. Many of the modern expectations of teachers are unrealistic.

418. Teachers should pick their battles.

419. School classes should be divided up (tracked) into ability groupings for teaching purposes.

420. No matter what you do, there are some students that just won't want to, or are incapable of learning a particular subject matter.

421. Sometimes, you have to remove some students from the class or the school so the other students can learn.

A parent might say:

422. There is no such thing as a stupid question.

423. Teachers should never appear upset with his students.

424. If the average test grade on an exam is low, it's the teacher's fault.

425. When teachers receive tenure, they become less likely to give their full effort to teaching.

A speaker at a professional development workshop might say:

426. In order to teach effectively, teachers must have a good relationship with their students.

427. Every student is talented at something.

428. Teachers communicate conscious and unconscious messages that are sexist and racist.

429. Teachers should document the interventions they have attempted to help struggling students.

A politician might say:

430. Parents have the right to homeschool their children in whatever way they see fit within the laws and regulations of the state and the board of education.

431. School districts should be able to teach students from low income families just as well as students from middle class or upper class families.

432. Teachers should be paid based on their students' achievement as measured by standardized tests.

433. Students should get paid for good grades.

434. Teachers' unions protect lazy and ineffective teachers.

435. Charter schools can teach more effectively than regular public schools.

436. Prayer should be allowed in schools.

437. Teachers should be allowed to carry concealed guns in school to protect students.

An administrator might say:

438. Teachers should not share much about their personal lives with their students.

439. Under no circumstances should a teacher touch a student.

440. Teachers need to be held accountable for their work to improve the achievement of all students.

441. Teachers should comply with school policies regardless of whether they think the policies make sense.

A union representative might say:

442. Teachers should not answer student and parent texts/e-mails/calls during the evening and weekends.

443. Teachers should not do anything beyond what their contract requires without getting compensated.

444. No matter what a teacher has done, if he is being considered for dismissal, he deserves union representation and due process.

445. The only way that a school or school system can be successfully reformed is by collaborating with the teacher's union.

A college professor might say:

446. If there are unequal testing or grade results in a teacher's class that fall along gender lines, the classroom teacher should attempt to counteract this disparity.

447. If there are unequal results in a teacher's class that fall along racial lines, the classroom teacher should attempt to counteract this disparity.

448. Teachers should learn the slang or the cultural language variations their students use.

449. If there is a dominant language that a teacher's students speak, that teacher should learn at least some of that language.

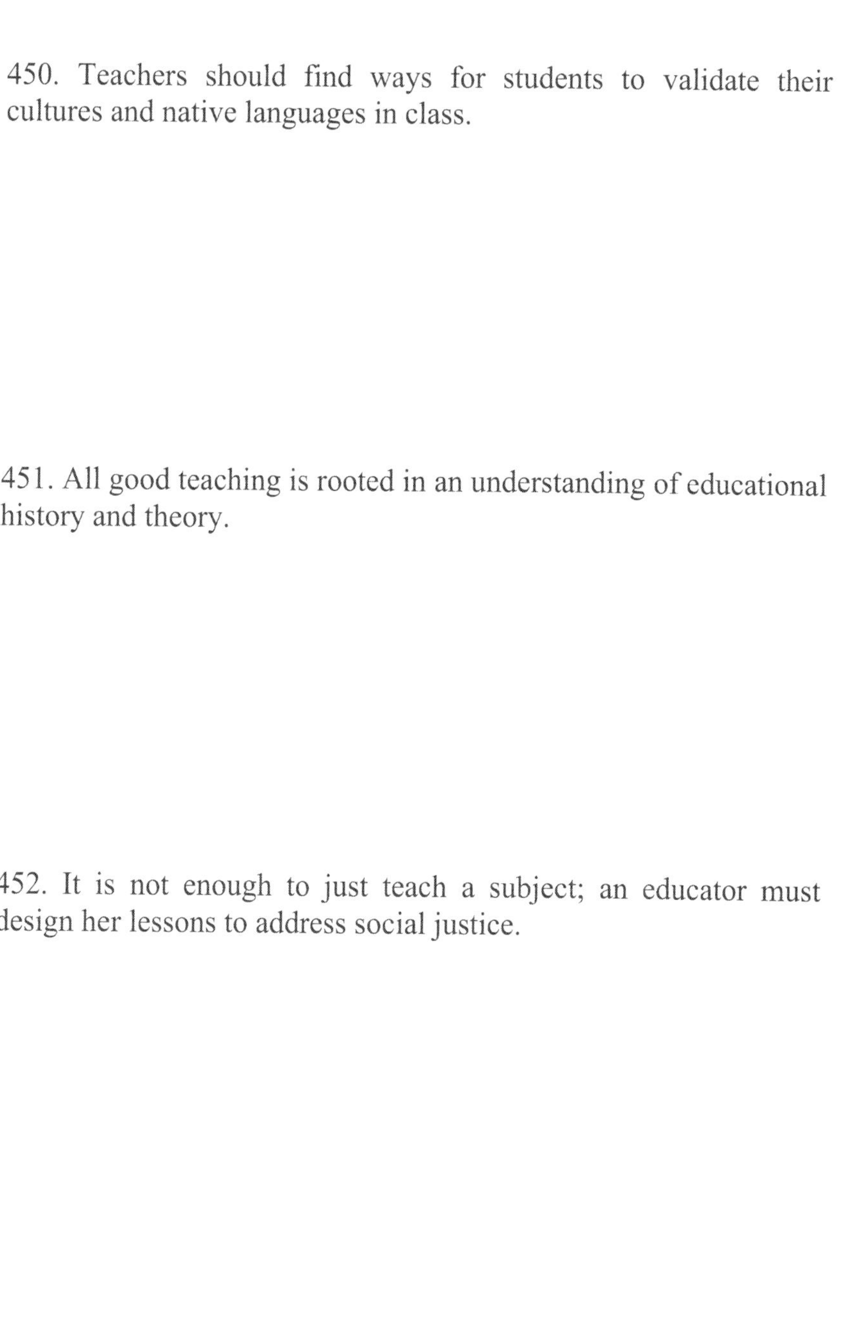

450. Teachers should find ways for students to validate their cultures and native languages in class.

451. All good teaching is rooted in an understanding of educational history and theory.

452. It is not enough to just teach a subject; an educator must design her lessons to address social justice.

Chapter 5

Would You Rather?

I grew up in a family where I was expected to ask and answer open-ended questions from an early age. This was particularly important to my father who was raised in a family that was full of very rigid political thinkers -- dissenting opinions were not encouraged. Relatives have also told me that a focus on discussion and debate is a key trait of cultural Judaism. I haven't spent time with families of every cultural background, but I'm pretty sure that Jews don't have a monopoly on arguing with each other.

I can say that my interest in all types of questioning is a direct result of my upbringing. I failed to develop a sense of a taboo topic since no discussion subjects were off-limits. I was accustomed to asking and answering questions on any issue at any time, and I relished those opportunities. Unfortunately for me, growing up without any boundaries to discussion topics had real and sometimes negative consequences for my social interactions. I was compelled to ask everyone I met probing and personal questions. I was also slow to learn that strangers sometimes shut down when asked direct and personal questions.

A personal question can elicit awkward responses from people you know well, let alone near strangers. The trick, I found, was that if the query came from a book, it opened more doors and minds. "The Book of Questions" by Gregory Stock, was my number one resource in college for starting discussions with friends and acquaintances. There's nothing like a late night dorm room conversation about whether one could urinate in front of others or go to a slaughterhouse and kill a cow to eat. Since that book was instrumental in my effort to get others to share their thoughts and feelings, I knew that I could write a book to help teachers engage in the same process with their chosen profession.

Would you lend pencils to your students? It seems like an easy question but an individual's answer reveals a great deal about what a teacher is trying to accomplish. If the goal is strictly to transmit content, giving out writing implements makes sense -- a teacher would want to remove any impediment to learning the material. If the goal is to encourage more social/emotional growth, providing pencils might create an unhealthy learned dependence. And if there's some sort of hybrid solution (using a shoe as collateral, limiting the amount of pencil loans), then that creates an administrative task which cuts into a teacher's instructional time.

Would you rather give an explanation that is so long that some students get bored or so short that some students are confused? Many teacher questions come down to whether a choice is good for the students or for you. For instance, it would probably help your students succeed if you tutored them in the evenings, but that would obviously take away from your social life and personal time. A whole other set of teacher questions address issues and choices that privilege one set of students over another. In every class, some students get the instructions and material quickly while others need more time. The question at the beginning of the paragraph is a good example of making a choice that actively helps one group while simultaneously hurting another.

If I explain something rapidly, the quick learning group will be satisfied and engaged, leaving the slower group confused. Taking my time to go over everything will help the students who need the extra help, but the quicker students might get restless or cause trouble. The other drawback of a slower method is that it takes time away from the entire class to practice the new material. In many of these teacher choices, time is the currency you are spending or saving when considering the conflicting needs of different groups and individuals.

The overarching conundrum is figuring out how to create a course that rewards more than one type of learner. I perpetually struggle with whether I'd rather have my students' grades be more reflective of their effort or their understanding of the material.

If I'm teaching physics, it seems like I should ultimately evaluate the degree to which my students have mastered the subject, and that would point towards tests as the most influential component. But, I also feel strongly that I should reward diligence, especially for those who struggle with the subject. This approach to incentivizing effort suggests a system with points for homework completion and large projects.

I have had successes and failures with both approaches. Sometimes, students have earned acceptable grades after appearing to learn very little, and other years (with differently-weighted categories), it has been personally troubling to see the sheer devastation in students who tried their hardest but failed to earn the grade they wanted. So, would you rather set up a grading system in which some students get grades they didn't deserve, or one that can fail students who tried but never master the material? Or, is that a false choice?

This section offers future and current teachers a series of dichotomies in the form of questions and scenarios based on my experience, but there is always the possibility that: (a) The dichotomy is false and excludes other options (b) the framework or the question doesn't apply to the context of your situation, or (c) You need to develop critical questions yourself depending on your background, experience and situation. In other words, you have to also question my questions and not just answer them.

Would You Rather…?

501. Would you rather have a fulfilling teaching career and only a partially fulfilling private life, or would you prefer a partially fulfilling teaching career and a fully fulfilling private life? Obviously, we'd all want to have both, but what if you had to choose?

502. Would you rather give an explanation that is too long and some students get bored or too short and some students are confused?

503. Would you rather deliver five so-so lessons in a day or have one outstanding class followed by more less-than-average ones?

504. Would you rather have a lesson that ended 10 minutes early or one in which you wish you had 10 more minutes? How would you handle each situation?

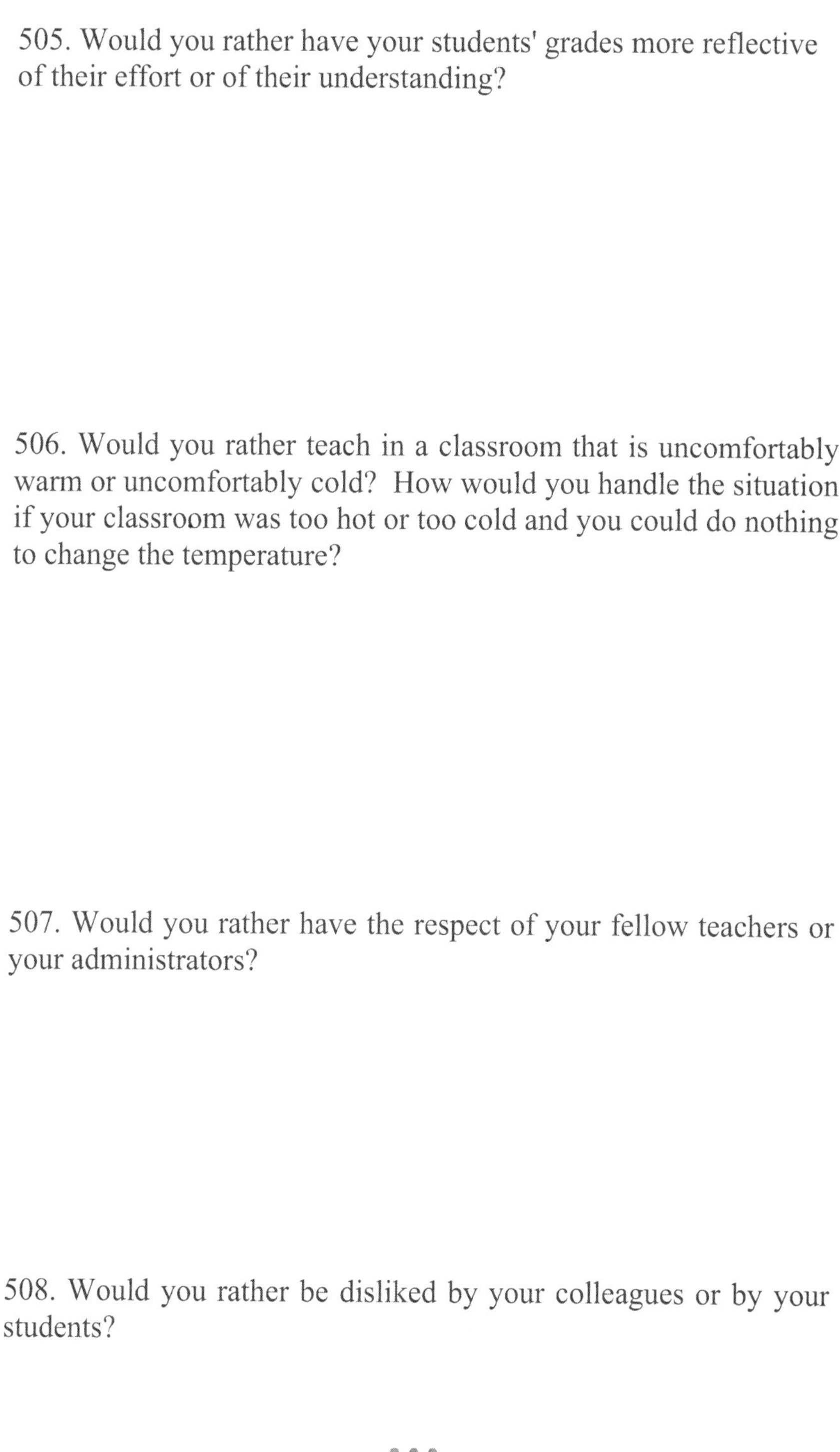

505. Would you rather have your students' grades more reflective of their effort or of their understanding?

506. Would you rather teach in a classroom that is uncomfortably warm or uncomfortably cold? How would you handle the situation if your classroom was too hot or too cold and you could do nothing to change the temperature?

507. Would you rather have the respect of your fellow teachers or your administrators?

508. Would you rather be disliked by your colleagues or by your students?

509. Would you rather have a quiet, bright, but overly compliant class, or an unruly and poorly performing class that has moments of brilliance?

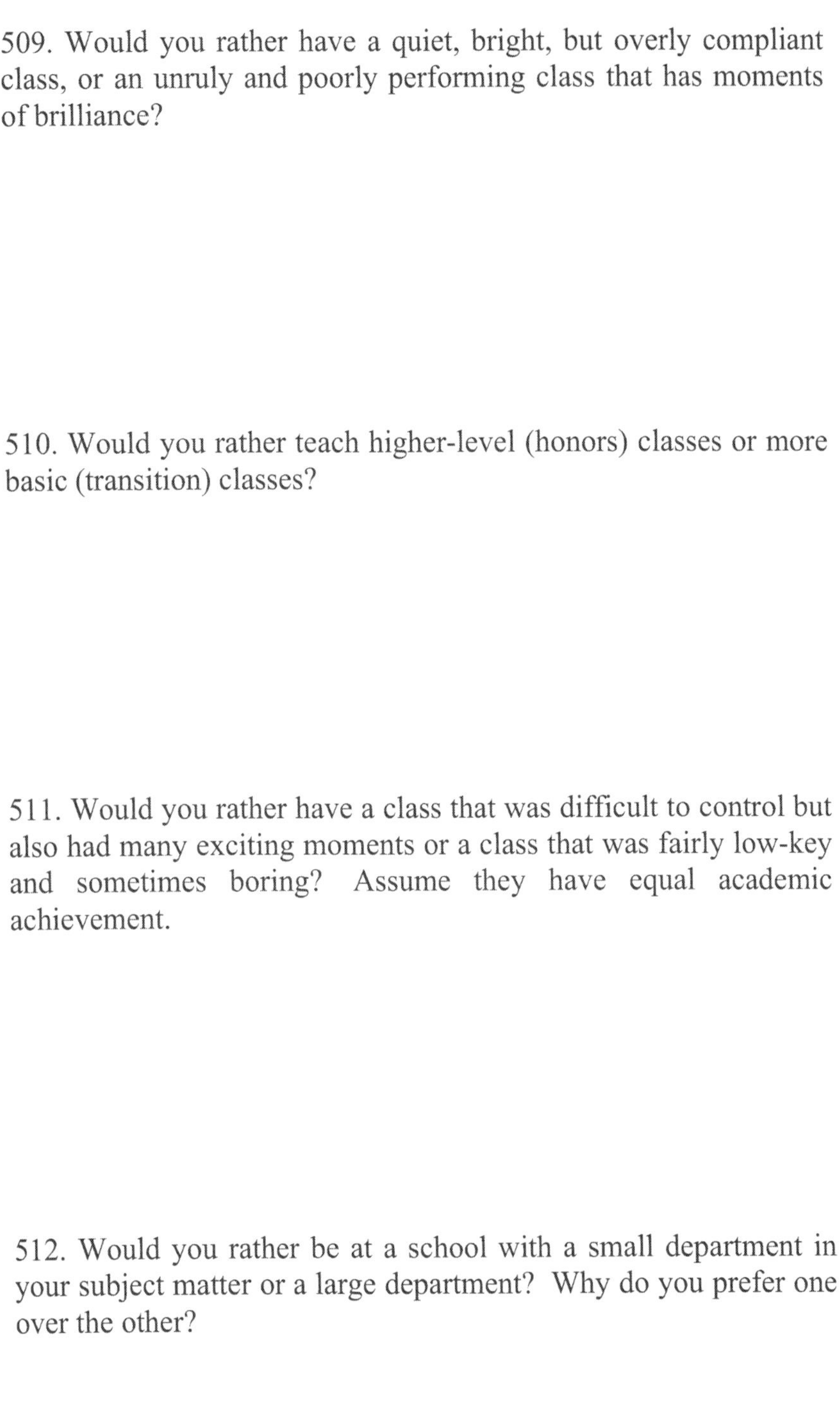

510. Would you rather teach higher-level (honors) classes or more basic (transition) classes?

511. Would you rather have a class that was difficult to control but also had many exciting moments or a class that was fairly low-key and sometimes boring? Assume they have equal academic achievement.

512. Would you rather be at a school with a small department in your subject matter or a large department? Why do you prefer one over the other?

513. Would you rather be at a school where the expectation is that you and your course-alike teachers do the exact same thing (common tests, teaching activities) or a school where you are expected to be more independent?

514. Would you rather teach at a variety of schools throughout your career or primarily stay at one? Assume that there is no need to change where you live.

515. Would you rather be an excellent teacher surrounded by mediocre colleagues or an average teacher surrounded by excellent colleagues?

516. Would you rather work with colleagues that are racist or sexist?

517. Would you rather be one of the younger teachers at your school or one of the older ones?

518. Would you rather that your students do better on standardized tests or the tests you create for your course?

519. Would you rather have slightly lower standardized test scores than your colleagues and slightly higher engagement/enjoyment among your students, or the reverse?

520. Would you rather teach at a school that has lots of "helicopter" parents who may be overinvolved in their child's education or at a school where parents tend to be under involved (or absent altogether)?

521. Would you rather be yelled at by an administrator or a parent?

522. Would you rather deal with a crying student or an angry student?

523. Would you rather have a stomach ache or head ache while teaching?

524. Would you rather be considered by students to be a hard grader though slightly unfair or an easy grader who gives kid the benefit of the doubt?

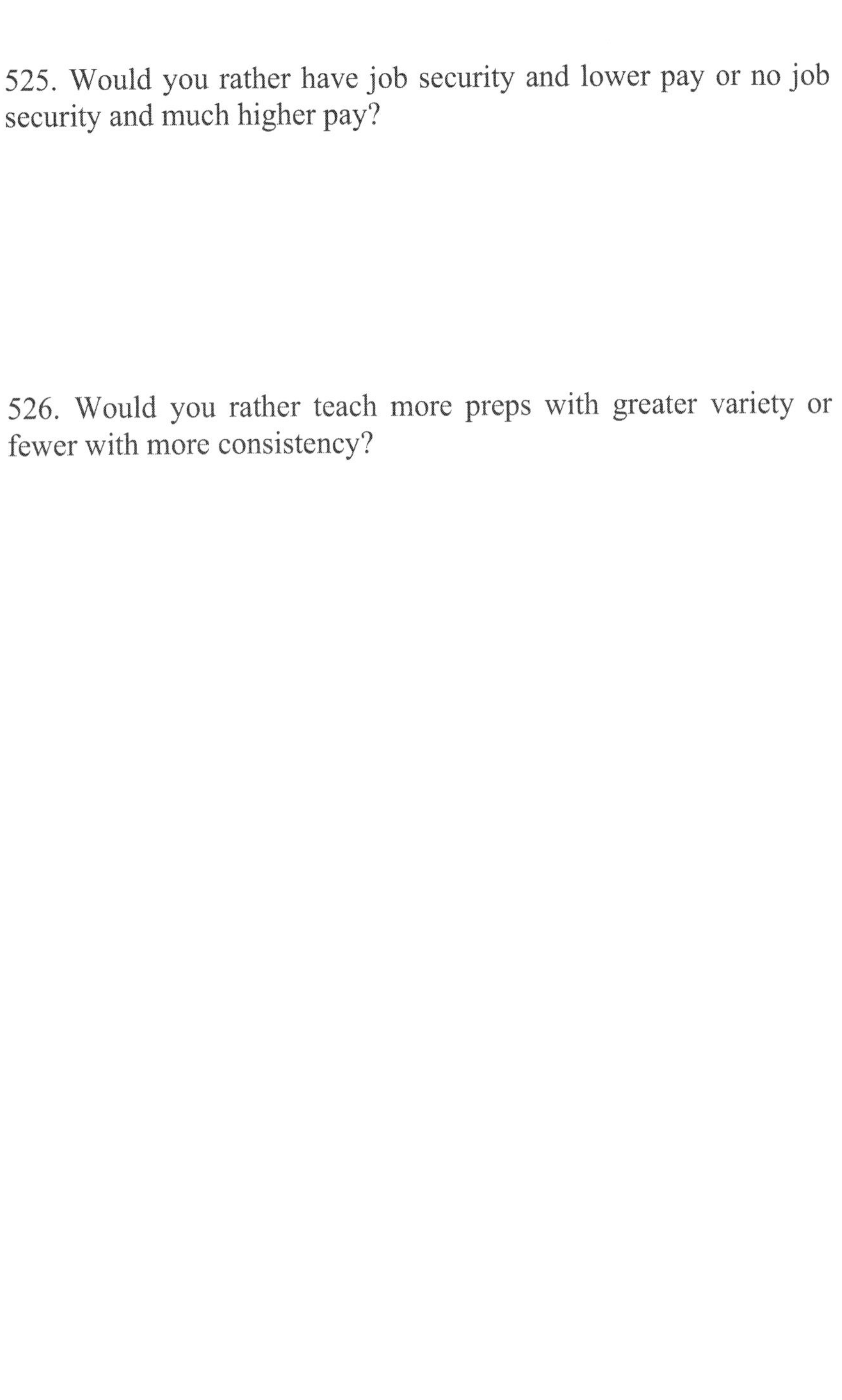

525. Would you rather have job security and lower pay or no job security and much higher pay?

526. Would you rather teach more preps with greater variety or fewer with more consistency?

Chapter 6

What If..?

How Would You Handle It grew out of this section, and it was conceived from my intense desire to help you make fewer mistakes than I made as a new teacher. Of course, you'll make your own mistakes and learn from them -- I just hope you won't be make as many as I did.

I thought I was going to be an amazing student teacher; I tutored extensively since I was twelve and worked in summer camps from the age of fifteen. I was a successful math and physics student and had been dreaming of teaching since my junior year of high school. Instead, to use the vernacular of the day, I sucked. There was just no other word for it in my mind at the time.

Not only was lesson planning significantly more difficult than I anticipated, I felt completely unprepared to manage a classroom of young people. It wasn't only that I was ineffective, I reacted so inappropriately to some situations that I could have endangered my quest to become a teacher. Once, I got so frustrated with a student constantly being in my physical space that I shoved him backwards. Another time, I reached out my hand to settle down two boys who were roughhousing in the lab. One of them was six inches taller than me, affecting where my hands touched his body. He later pulled my cooperating teacher aside to tell her that I touched him inappropriately near his butt.

Fortunately, both situations were resolved without ending my nascent career. Unfortunately, those teacher gaffes didn't put an end to my periodic cluelessness when it came to handling unforeseen events. One day during student teaching, my cooperating teacher was out for the day, and a substitute took her place. Close to the end of the period, a heated exchange erupted near the door between two boys. Just as the bell rang, they started to exchange punches while the class spilled into the hallway.

Now this was a situation that I *had* anticipated. I took off my teacher hat and imagined that I was back in high school on the wrestling mat, rapidly immobilizing one of the fighters in a headlock. Before I could revel in my ability to physically dominate this young man, I realized the tactical error I made; the other fighter started landing *unblocked* punches on the face of the student I was holding. Fortunately, a security guard soon came to grab the other student and end the fight. However, the damage had already been done -- my student had a broken nose and a bloodied face.

The role I played in "resolving" this altercation is probably the best example of the "what if..." errors I made in my first few years of teaching. I jumped into a classroom situation that I thought I could handle and chose the best course of action based on previous experience. But instead of making the situation better, the student was worse off, and I went home feeling guilty about the consequences of my mistake.

Since then, I have taught thousands of students and worked with hundreds of pre-service teachers. The future teachers I have followed always get most nervous before they begin student teaching and want me to tell them that everything is going to be OK. Instead, I tell them that they will be terrible -- they just have to try to be less terrible each day.

As bad as that sounds, it's the message that prospective and new teachers tell me helps them the most. It frees them up to try new techniques in class and not beat themselves up when it doesn't go perfectly. They analyze their interactions with students and the class without the oppressive notion that there is one true path for all educators. And it is the mantra that I repeated to myself in my first few years of teaching: be less terrible each day and stop worrying about being perfect right away.

I have focused on student transgressions, but some of these "what if..." situations aren't the result of any student misbehavior. A good example occurred during a morning class in my first year of teaching. It involved a group of students similar to the period five class that I featured in the introduction of the book, but because half the students had IEPs, the class was co-taught with a special education teacher.

The special education teacher and I had an excellent working relationship. At the moment she was in the front of the classroom explaining a problem on the overhead projector, and I was checking in the students' homework. Suddenly, she started screaming and ran out of the room.

I have always felt that people irrationally fear mice. In the presence of these miniscule creatures, they turn into clumsy and panicked elephants (who, by the way, are *not* afraid of mice). In addition to my co-teacher losing her cool when she saw the grey furry rodent in our classroom, a third of the students were in the back of the room shrieking like they were witnessing a bear attack.

My surprise at the sudden events changed to annoyance because the students continued to linger and stare. It took me a while to realize exactly what was going on. Most mice sightings are fleeting. But this mouse was dragging a khaki colored plastic rectangle through the middle of the classroom. Rodent poison, as I learned later, is not allowed in schools -- something about how children may lick the floors. Instead, educational institutions use glue traps.

Glue traps are incredibly sticky and baited to attract rodents. Once stuck, mice desperately try to free themselves, often chewing off their own body parts to escape. This little guy had his back feet attached to the trap and was army-crawling through the middle of the classroom.

I presumed that I could demonstrate my disdain for musophobics (those who irrationally fear mice) and impress the entire class by at least knocking the glue trap under the desk until a buildings and ground crewmember could "deal" with it. I strutted over to the mouse/trap combo and gave a carefully measured kick. I thought I had swiftly resolved the situation until I discovered that the glue trap *and* the mouse had become stuck to my foot.

Now it was my turn to panic. While the mouse was still writhing on the glue trap attached to my foot, I started shaking violently and making noises like I was wild animal. I went from the self-appointed savior to hapless clown in a matter of seconds. My unintentional act had at least one benefit -- everybody came back into class to see what was going on. My flailing finally dislodged the trap, and I had all eyes on me to reset the class. While I'll never kick a glue trap again, I learned that doing something ridiculous can refocus a group of students. I actually reused this technique with great success later that year as I jump-started an apathetic honors class by running across the tops of their desks and chanting gibberish.

I left student teaching with a better method for breaking up fights (use a bent arm on one kid while using a stiff arm on the other), I inadvertently discovered an insane way to deal with mice (and other whole-class distractions), but I was stumped when I witnessed what I thought was a drug deal going down in my 5th period algebra class (the same tightly packed space with Jeremy and Tanya).

I was going over the method for finding slope when I overheard some talking between Julian and Paul. The conversation surprised me because I had never observed Paul do much of anything given that he was usually withdrawn and inattentive. I once called his father to say that Paul wasn't doing any homework, but I got the sense that homework completion was the least of that family's problems. Julian was more social but had a dangerous edge to him. When he was on my side, he was a real ally to me as I taught, but if he felt crossed by anyone, he was willing to fight. He and I had also talked privately about the economic and emotional effects of growing up fatherless.

A short conversation between peers in a class like that didn't warrant a pause in my instruction, so I continued. Today, I am thankful for smart boards, but in 2001, my only option for displaying a worksheet was an overhead projector. That meant staring into a blinding light as I wrote with easy-to-smudge wet erase markers. It certainly wasn't graceful for me with bad handwriting and general physical awkwardness.

Moments after their initial conversation, I was pushing the absolute speed limit of my pupil dilation as I looked back and forth from the projector to the class when I saw Julian and Paul exchange something. I was fairly sure that Paul gave Julian money. Then I saw Julian give money to Paul, and that didn't make any sense -- why would a kid exchange money for money? We didn't have DVRs at the time but if we did, I would have felt like I was pressing the instant replay button over and over. While I moved on with the lesson, the images in my mind became clearer -- Paul gave Julian a twenty-dollar bill, and Julian gave Paul a few ones with a baggie inside.

Like the situation with Jeremy and Tanya, I couldn't think of anything to do, so I didn't do anything. All I could manage to do was add this question to my list of questions for pre-service teachers, "What would you do if you think you observe a drug deal occurring during class?"

As outrageous as some may seem, every single one of these "What if..?" situations has happened to a colleague, my wife or myself. One of the basic tenets of this book is that the worst possible time to think about how you would handle a situation is while it is actually happening. Even if my scenarios don't exactly match what unfolds in your future classroom, I feel confident in saying that the time put in reflecting on it now will pay off in the future. My college students will often text me excitedly about a "What if..." that happened to them in class, and we'll debrief how they handled it. I hope you find a sensitive and open-minded mentor who helps you reflect on these scenarios before you begin to teach. That's not to say that you'll be perfect after working through this book because: (a) something unexpected can always happen, (b) you don't know how you are actually going to respond until something is happening, and (c) reflecting on better ways to handle a situation is essential to balancing the roles of a teacher as instructor and facilitator of a positive environment. As you go through this process I expect you to *fail effectively* while you gradually learn from your mistakes, understand yourself better and fully integrate the reflective process.

What would you do if…?

One-on-one

601. A student asks to see you outside of class. Before beginning, he asks you to not tell anybody what he is about to tell you.

602. A student that you have suspected going through various transitions asks to see you after school. After some small talk, he tells you that he is gay. He has not told his parents but he wants you to sponsor a LGBT club in the school. He also asks for your help in getting his parents to understand.

If you are open to starting the LGBT club at school, would your answer change if your place of employment was generally homophobic, and past efforts to start a club were met with derision from faculty and students alike?

603. A girl asks to talk to you after class. She tells you that she's pregnant and wants you to help her figure out how to tell her family. She also wants you to help her find resources for an abortion.

604. You see a bruise on one of your students and you ask him about it after class. He acts uncomfortable talking about it but says it happened at practice. He senses that you are going to tell somebody and gets very angry with you. He says this has happened before (a teacher reporting a bruise), and all it did was get him in a lot of trouble at home.

Drugs

605. While going over a worksheet, you notice two students interacting in the back. One student hands a clear plastic bag of something to the other, and the second student hands back cash.

606. You notice one morning that a normally rambunctious and distracted student is very focused and placid. You also notice a strong aroma of marijuana when you go near her. Other students are starting to smell it and are mumbling that she must be high.

607. While students are working in groups you hear them talking about a huge party at a student's house because her parents will be gone. They are talking about bringing alcohol and drugs to the party.

608. After a class has left, you see a bag of white powder underneath the seat of a student you suspect is abusing drugs.

Race

609. You suspect that a student doesn't like you because of your race.

610. A student uses the n-word when talking to a peer. You are pretty sure that it was meant in a familiar way but you are not positive. Would the race of the speaker and listener matter?

611. You teach at a school with a pretty demographically diverse student body. While presenting a lesson, you ask for volunteers to answer a question. A number of students want to participate, and you call on one to give the first answer. Another who wanted to answer shouts out, "You're a racist. You didn't call on me because I'm black."

612. During a discussion, a student raises her hand and asks why your curriculum doesn't include many people who look like him.

Religion

613. One of your students is in the hospital and very sick. Another of your student raises her hand and asks to lead the class in a prayer.

614. While mentioning an upcoming school holiday, a student raises her hand and asks why other religions and religious holidays go unmentioned in schools.

615. You are planning a Halloween party, and a parent e-mails you to say that her child can't participate because celebrating Halloween is against their religion.

616. Your school expects you to lead the students through the pledge of allegiance each morning. One of your students refuses to participate because of the "under God" section.

Colleagues

617. A colleague and mentor wants you to focus on the curriculum but your assistant principal (and evaluator) wants you to spend more time on standardized test preparation.

618. You were hired by a school where most instruction is traditional and direct while you want to use more modern inquiry and progressive pedagogy.

619. A colleague teaching the same course is using all of your materials instead of creating his own. Would it matter if he gave you credit?

620. You have a department and/or colleagues who have very negative attitudes toward teaching and students.

621. Members of your department are hostile towards each other and make it their goal to get as many teachers as possible to take their side.

622. While the students are working on an activity, they start talking about a previous teacher they all had. You hear them say that the teacher was terrible and other cruel insults. You know that this teacher is particularly ineffective. You go over to redirect the group, but they get more riled up and demand to know what you think of that teacher before they return to their classroom work.

623. While students are working on an activity, you overhear one of them saying that another teacher made a negative comment about you because all of your students were trying to switch into his classes.

624. You are teaching class and a colleague walks in. That teacher observes student behavior that you tolerate in class, but that colleague does not. That colleague corrects the behavior in front of you.

625. You discover that one of your office mates is having an affair with an administrator. Both your colleague and the administrator are married to other people.

Administrators

626. A troubled student ended up becoming pregnant and missed a lot of school at the end of the year. She didn't earn a passing grade. An administrator pressures you to raise a student's grade to passing because, "she has had a hard year."

627. You feel that your department chair/immediate supervisor suddenly has something against you, which may be unrelated to teaching. You have always had good evaluations but the most recent one by her is very negative and nitpicky.

628. An administrator looks at your grade book and decides that you are giving too many Ds and Fs. He instructs you to raise the grades of your students across the board.

629. Your school has a policy for students to wear IDs at all times. However, this policy is rarely enforced and your department chair also feels that it is not important. As a new teacher, you want to follow the rules and get lots of resistance from students. One day when you are bringing your students through the hallway, your principal sees non-compliance and pulls you aside to say that you need to insist on your students wearing IDs. You increase your efforts in class, meet more resistance and decide to refer the infractions to the dean of discipline. The dean says that the lack of compliance is more reflective of your deficiencies in behavior management and refuses to discipline the students.

630. You are untenured and running a successful club for the school. The new assistant principal who directly oversees the clubs and activities is an obstructionist who is making it very difficult for you to do your extra-curricular activity. You have tried to have a rational discussion with the assistant principal and she threatens to write you up for insubordination. You are thinking about going to tell the principal about what is happening.

Parents

631. You are out to eat at a restaurant with friends when a parent approaches you and wants to talk about classroom issues with his child.

632. You have been in contact with a parent about her child who has disruptive behavior in class. The mother of the child requests to sit in class to observe her child. While the mother is there, the child acts even worse than normal. The mother tries to get the student to behave and he ignores her. The mother starts to beat the child in front of the class.

633. During a parent –teacher conference, a parent starts flirting with you.

634. During a conversation with a parent on the phone, a parent threatens to sue you and the school if you don't change her child's grade.

Defiance of Authority

635. While going over homework with the class, you see that one student is not checking his homework. In fact, he is flossing his teeth. You go over quietly and ask him to stop. He loudly accuses you of not supporting proper hygiene.

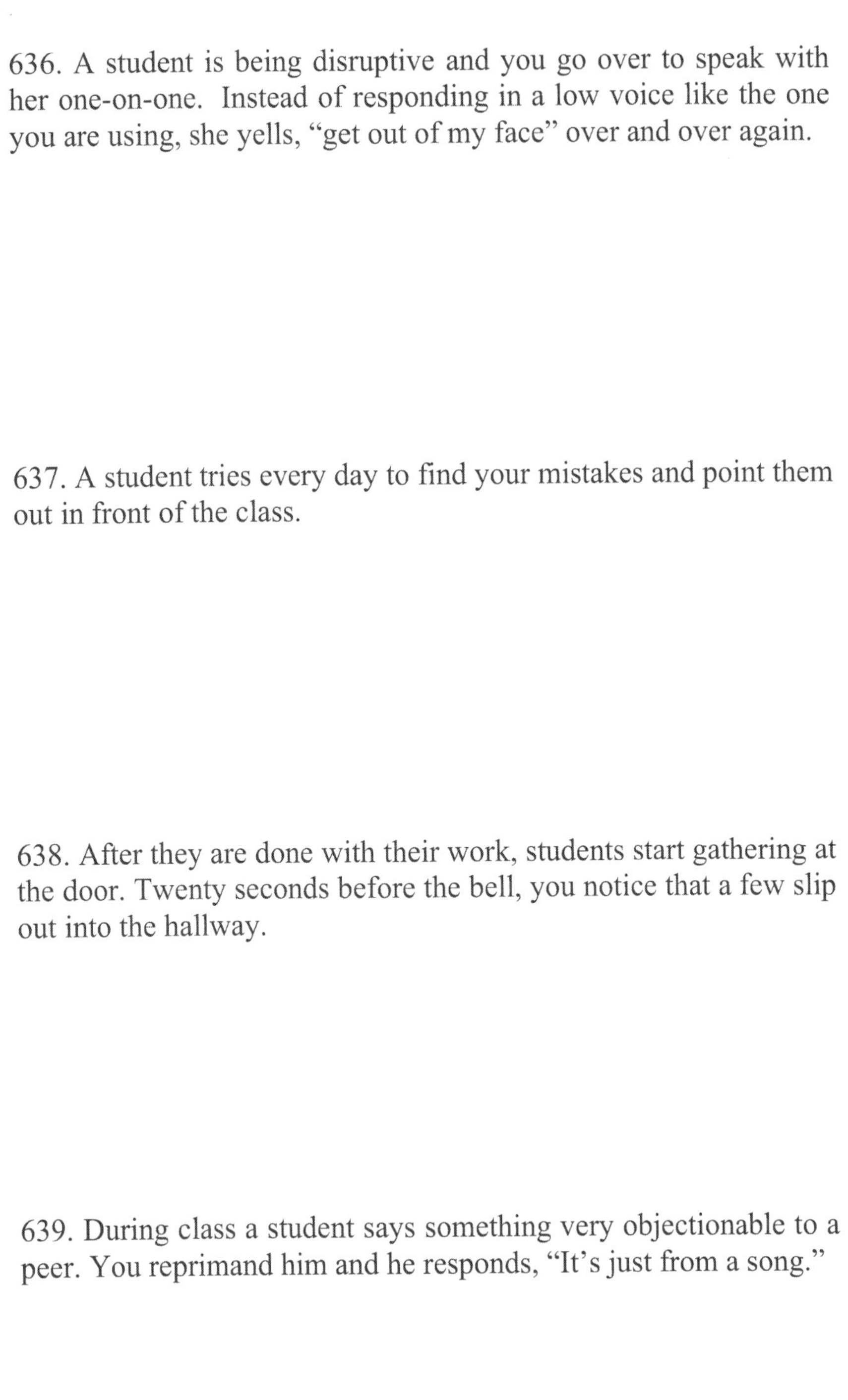

636. A student is being disruptive and you go over to speak with her one-on-one. Instead of responding in a low voice like the one you are using, she yells, “get out of my face” over and over again.

637. A student tries every day to find your mistakes and point them out in front of the class.

638. After they are done with their work, students start gathering at the door. Twenty seconds before the bell, you notice that a few slip out into the hallway.

639. During class a student says something very objectionable to a peer. You reprimand him and he responds, “It’s just from a song.”

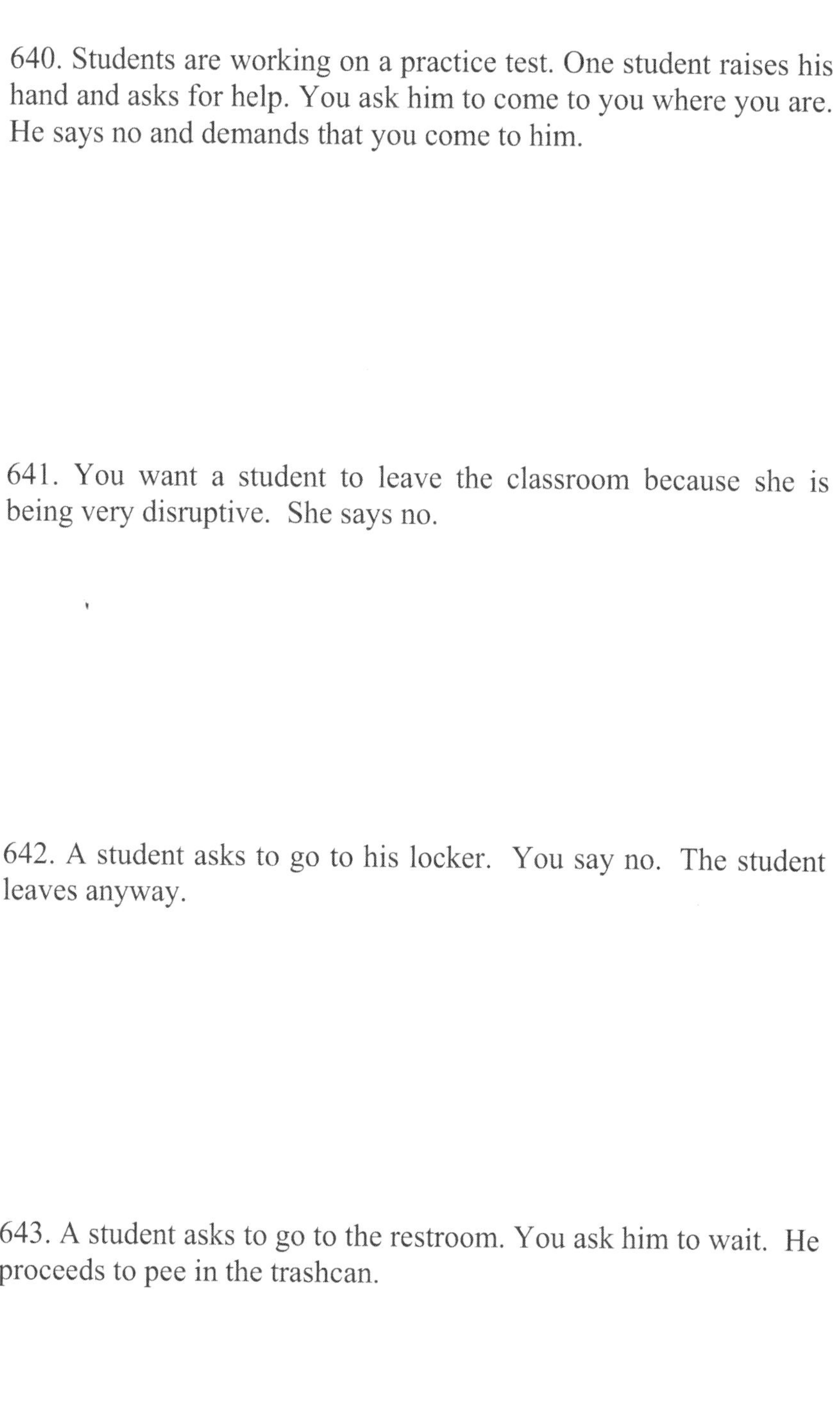

640. Students are working on a practice test. One student raises his hand and asks for help. You ask him to come to you where you are. He says no and demands that you come to him.

641. You want a student to leave the classroom because she is being very disruptive. She says no.

642. A student asks to go to his locker. You say no. The student leaves anyway.

643. A student asks to go to the restroom. You ask him to wait. He proceeds to pee in the trashcan.

Defiance of Authority (continued)

644. At the end of the period, you are talking to one student about her disruptive behavior during class. Her best friend is standing next to her and telling her to just ignore you and walk away.

645. A student likes to find creative ways to "flip you off." He uses his middle finger when he points at things and comes up to you with his middle finger raised to complain about an injury.

Sexual content

646. You are a female teacher and a student tells you that because of his culture, he can't respect women as teachers.

647. You are just beginning a lesson and trying to get the class to settle down. A student shouts out that you have a nice ass. What would you do if you didn't know who said it?

648. What would you do if you find yourself sexually attracted to one of your students or you become aware that one of your students is sexually attracted to you?

649. While explaining an assignment, you notice two students are physically very close. As you continue to talk, you see that one of them is rubbing a private part of the other.

650. You really feel like you have reached a student. At the beginning of the year you had a lot of conflict but now you have finally connected, and the two of you have a good understanding of each other. As he is walking out of class before a long weekend, he swoops in quickly and gives you a hug, pressing his chest against yours.

651. You notice a student is staring directly at you. Then you notice the student is masturbating.

652. You find an opened note on the ground after class. You notice the student-author wrote that he is going to have sex with somebody much younger than himself.

653. You walk into the bathroom and hear what sounds like two people having sex in a stall.

Safety

654. At end of the day, you find a gang sign scratched into a desk. You are not sure who did it but you know the five students who sit in that seat during the day.

655. After you disciplined a student in the beginning of the year, there has always been tension between you and that student. One day, she was particularly unruly and you had to verbally discipline her a few times. At the end of class, when students are milling about, she looks at you. Then she makes her hand look like a gun, pulls the "trigger" and says, "BANG."

656. You are doing an activity with supplies. You see a student take some of the supplies and put them in her backpack.

657. While the students are working quietly on an assignment, two students sitting next to each other start arguing. One is accusing the other of stealing her phone and is threatening to start a fight. Would your response change if the two students were good friends?

658. You are by the door saying goodbye to your students after class. As one student is leaving, he tucks his shirt in and you see a glint of metal at the small of his back and think it could be a weapon.

659. In the middle of teaching a lesson, an administrator calls you to the door. She tells you that the student who is absent that period died of a gunshot wound the night before. She tells you to inform his classmates.

Individual vs. Class needs

660. There's a student who has not shown much interest in your class so far this year. You know that for whatever reason, she cannot or will not come before or after school for help. For some reason, she starts asking questions in class one day. However, this is material that has been covered already. The rest of the class appears to grasp it and is getting restless.

661. A student in your class has a disability that makes it very difficult for him to interact normally with other students. Well intentioned or not, his comments make other students uncomfortable and sometimes the entire class gets angry with him. The student seems to enjoy being a pariah.

662. A student is very bright and does everything he can to monopolize your attention during class discussions. He blurts out answers and gets upset when you don't call on him. Would your response to this situation change if you knew the student had a disability that impairs his social functioning?

663. A very committed student asks a lot of questions in class. The problem is that many of the questions are obvious or at least easy for the rest of the class to answer. The class gets frustrated every time the student raises his hand to ask a question.

Student vs. Student

664. While transitioning from one activity to another, a student passes gas loudly. This begins a ruckus and students start shouting about how smelly the classroom is.

665. Throughout the year, you have been aware of a student who has less than ideal hygiene. One day he comes in and is particularly smelly. The other students notice and start to complain. The students next to him shout out that they won't sit next to him because he stinks.

666. During an activity a group is arguing with each other a lot. They insist that the problem is that you picked groups for them instead of allowing them to pick their own group members.

667. Two students that you know to be friends are having an argument. You are not sure if they are actually mad at each other. One of them turns to you and says, "She's bullying me – you should send her to her dean." Would your response change if you knew they were not friends?

668. You have a student in your class who you know often gets into trouble. During group work, you overhear her talking about stealing something from somebody the day before.

669. At the end of a large group project one of your students pulls you aside to say that she basically did all the work and doesn't feel that the other members deserve credit. When you talk to the other members of the group, they insist they did their fair share.

Classroom Choices

670. You spend a lot of time designing an activity that is based on a method you learned in college rather than the normal "cookbook" sort of lesson. You are nervous because you aren't sure how the students will react to this alternate way of learning. After you explain the activity, the students start the activity and many are frustrated. Some yell out, "this is stupid" and, "I hate this."

671. You are in the middle of an important activity and the fire alarm goes off. The activity can only be done in class but when you return after the "all clear," there isn't enough time to finish. All of your other classes finished the activity.

672. A lesson ends 20 minutes early.

673. During a test you see a student who you are pretty sure is glancing around at other tests.

674. You are about to start a test and a student comes up to you and says, “I can’t take this because I’m not ready.”

Would your reply be different if that student missed the day before?

What if she was in class yesterday but not the two days before that?

What if the student had some personal crisis the night before?

What about any other kind of excuse?

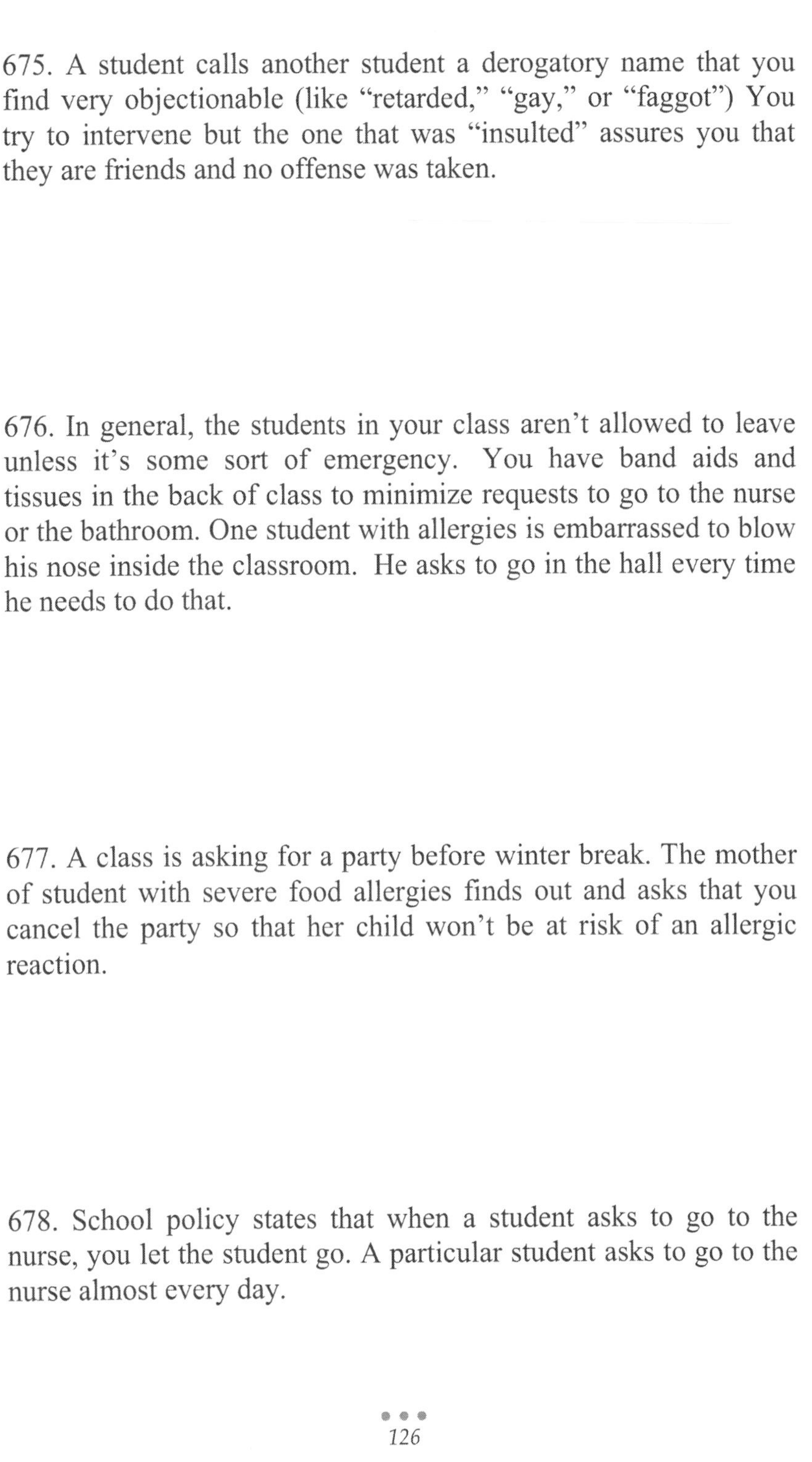

675. A student calls another student a derogatory name that you find very objectionable (like “retarded,” “gay,” or “faggot”) You try to intervene but the one that was “insulted” assures you that they are friends and no offense was taken.

676. In general, the students in your class aren’t allowed to leave unless it’s some sort of emergency. You have band aids and tissues in the back of class to minimize requests to go to the nurse or the bathroom. One student with allergies is embarrassed to blow his nose inside the classroom. He asks to go in the hall every time he needs to do that.

677. A class is asking for a party before winter break. The mother of student with severe food allergies finds out and asks that you cancel the party so that her child won’t be at risk of an allergic reaction.

678. School policy states that when a student asks to go to the nurse, you let the student go. A particular student asks to go to the nurse almost every day.

Personal

679. You have a class that enjoys getting you off track. What if you are explaining something and they ask: your dating status? Your sexual preference and history? Your religion? Where you live? Your drug and alcohol use in high school?

680. During a little speech on preparing the students for their futures, instead of saying the word success, you slip and say, "sex." How would you handle other inadvertent suggestive or inappropriate comments that you make?

681. You start the day not feeling well. As the day goes on, your stomach gets worse. After lunch, you are presenting a lesson and you think you are about to throw up.

682. What if you have to pass gas and there is no way for you to leave the classroom?

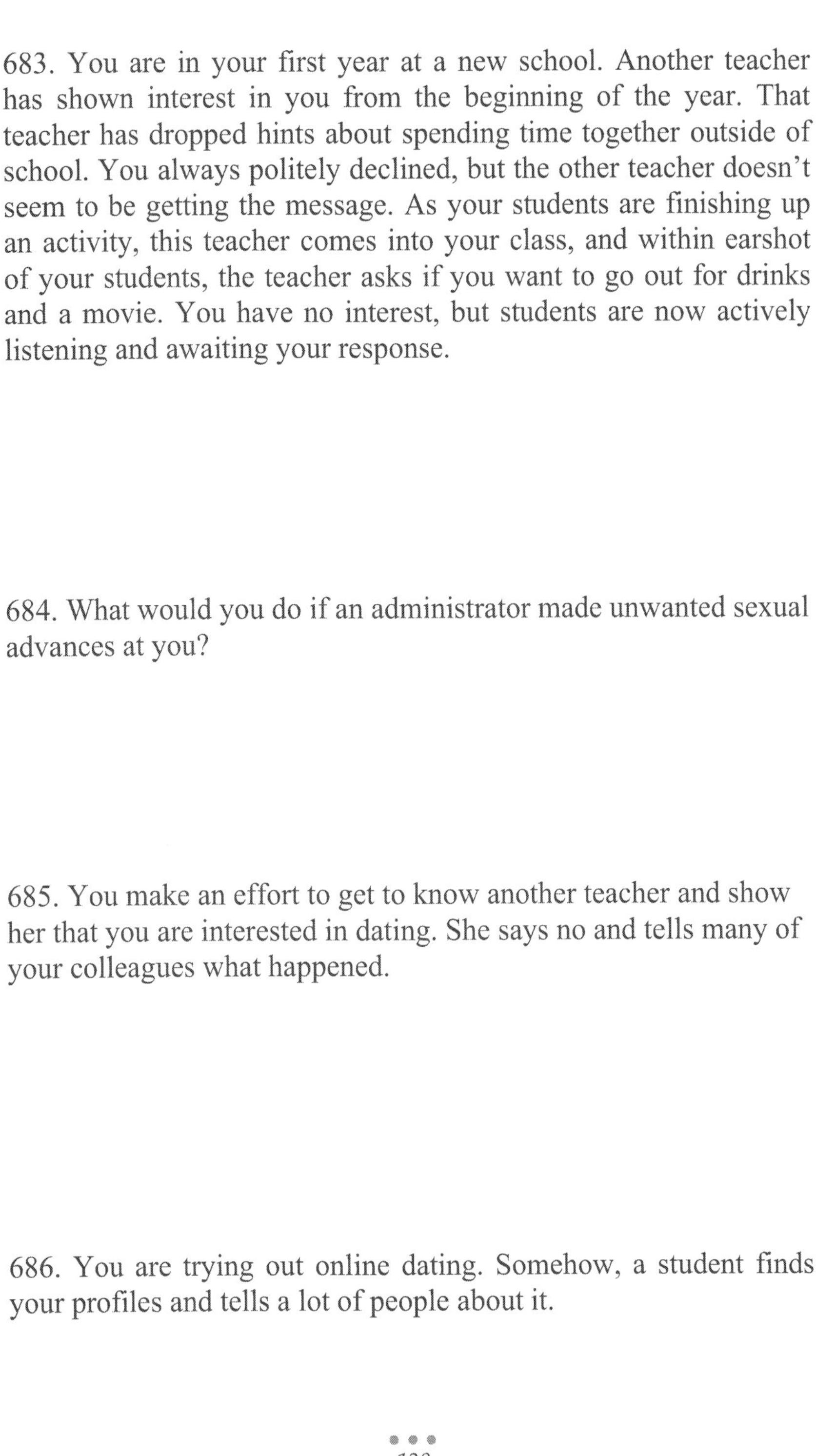

683. You are in your first year at a new school. Another teacher has shown interest in you from the beginning of the year. That teacher has dropped hints about spending time together outside of school. You always politely declined, but the other teacher doesn't seem to be getting the message. As your students are finishing up an activity, this teacher comes into your class, and within earshot of your students, the teacher asks if you want to go out for drinks and a movie. You have no interest, but students are now actively listening and awaiting your response.

684. What would you do if an administrator made unwanted sexual advances at you?

685. You make an effort to get to know another teacher and show her that you are interested in dating. She says no and tells many of your colleagues what happened.

686. You are trying out online dating. Somehow, a student finds your profiles and tells a lot of people about it.

Chapter 7

Conduct of Another Teacher

There is a tennis and racquetball club not far from my childhood home that seemed elite to me at the time, and it's not something my parents would have considered joining when I was young. They both worked at modest paying social service jobs, and this kind of club was beyond their means and outside their social sphere. Growing up, I visited it a few times with friends and always thought the members there reflected a kind of modern day aristocracy. I was sure that the other kids' parents never struggled in jobs with low salaries in order to serve others, as mine had.

Then a funny thing happened when I became an adolescent. Our household financial picture improved, and our family discovered that we shared a love of racquetball. We became members of the tennis and racquetball club that I used to deride and played there frequently. Strangely, I was still not able to shake the feeling that the *other* members were privileged snobs. I knew this by looking at them.

Later as a newly married but childless man, I scoffed at parents who took their kids to fast food restaurants. It seemed like the ultimate lower class activity: laziness combined with an indifference to the health of their progeny. It shouldn't surprise you that in less than two years, *I* was that parent bringing his children to McDonalds for fries and nuggets. Still, the other families there looked low class to me.

I share personal prejudices with you to assert that judgment comes very easily to all of us. In fact, I don't ever believe someone when they claim to not judge others at all. To truly not judge others, you would have to have no core values, and that would imply living in some strange universe where all actions can be rationalized. I have argued that many classroom decisions are indeed justifiable from a certain perspective, and I'm using these "other teacher" scenarios in this section to help you figure out your classroom values.

Let's say that a veteran teacher says to you, "Whether they learn or not, I still get paid." That may seem repugnant to an aspiring teacher, and you may swear never to utter a similar statement. But, it's at least worth considering why the veteran teacher would say that. Did he start off young and idealistic like you? Did some series of events lead to this sentiment? Perhaps this teacher does care, but talks this way to insulate himself from the pain of failing to reach some students. Teaching is a very personal endeavor and it wouldn't surprise me that teachers have various defense mechanisms to protect their feelings.

Or maybe he just doesn't care anymore, and that makes you wonder about the merits of tenure and other protections built into teacher contracts. The point is that judging and *dismissing* the actions of the teachers won't help you become a reflective teacher. It's worth wondering why other teachers do what they do for two reasons: it helps you figure out your values as a teacher and may help you deal with the creeping cynicism that some teachers experience.

Let's say that you know a teacher who occasionally recounts self-deprecating and funny stories about his dating life to his class. The kids enjoy the stories and always ask for more. Is that OK with you? Can you see yourself doing something similar? If the conduct of this teacher troubles you, why is that? What is acceptable to share with your students? Is what's acceptable for other teachers to do the same as what's acceptable for you? What would be the purpose of sharing personal information with students? What are the perils? And lastly, would your opinion of a teacher's tendency to self-disclose change if he were openly gay, extremely political, religious or atheist?

Let's imagine that a teacher you're observing has a student who frequently does not listen to her directions. One day after giving specific directions, the student asks a question about something that was clearly explained already, and the teacher refuses to answer the student. When judging this teacher, you'll have to grapple with the educational adage that "There is no such thing as a stupid question." Is the teacher right to refuse a question? Does the teacher's tone matter when refusing? Are students justified to say something like, "You're the teacher -- it's your job to answer our questions!" How might you respond to a similar situation? How would you respond if a parent accused you of not answering his child's questions? What's to be gained from making students seek their own answers to questions? What are the dangers of turning a student away who is looking for some kind of help?

In the previous two paragraphs, I modeled the way I might think through some of these examples of another teacher's conduct. That's not to say that my way is best, but doing a deeper analysis is clearly better practice than passing judgment and not learning from the experience. Once you are a teacher, it's helpful to continue to ask yourself why you make the decisions you do in class. If you end up with "that kid" who always asks for a private explanation, will your response always be the same to that student? If it depends, what should it depend on? After reflecting on a series of similar interactions with various students, should there be some sort of consistency in how you handle inattentive students? Or is it appropriate to tailor the response to each student?

As I stated in the introduction of the book, the key is to never stop the process of analysis and self-reflection. I find that I am at my worst as a teacher when I start slacking off in this area, and that's one more reason why a career as a teacher is so challenging. You would think that as you gain more experience, you can become less anxious about day-to-day preparations. That's true to a large extent, but that same process of relaxing about today can lead to passivity towards thinking about what happened yesterday and what you should do tomorrow. I encourage you to use the descriptions of other teachers' actions in this chapter to sharpen your sense of purpose as a teacher and skills as a reflective educator.

What is your opinion about the conduct of the teachers described below?

Boundaries

701. A teacher is struggling with a student who seeks attention by annoying other students. The teacher pulls this kid aside and asks what he wants his peers to think about him. He responds that he would want others to know that he is a religious Christian but admits that he sometimes annoys other kids when they ignore him. The teacher asks the student if Jesus would approve of that behavior.

702. A teacher is working hard to understand what's troubling a certain student. The student isn't forthcoming, the counselor isn't sure and the parents are hard to reach. The teacher ends up explaining his observations to the student's friends and asks them if they know what's bothering this student.

703. A teacher is trying to relate to the violence his class has experienced in their daily lives and makes up a story for a test about a shootout between gang members.

704. A teacher starts off extremely passionate about education but struggles in an unsupportive environment throughout his first two years of teaching. He resorts to swearing regularly at the students and seems proud to have found a technique for controlling his class.

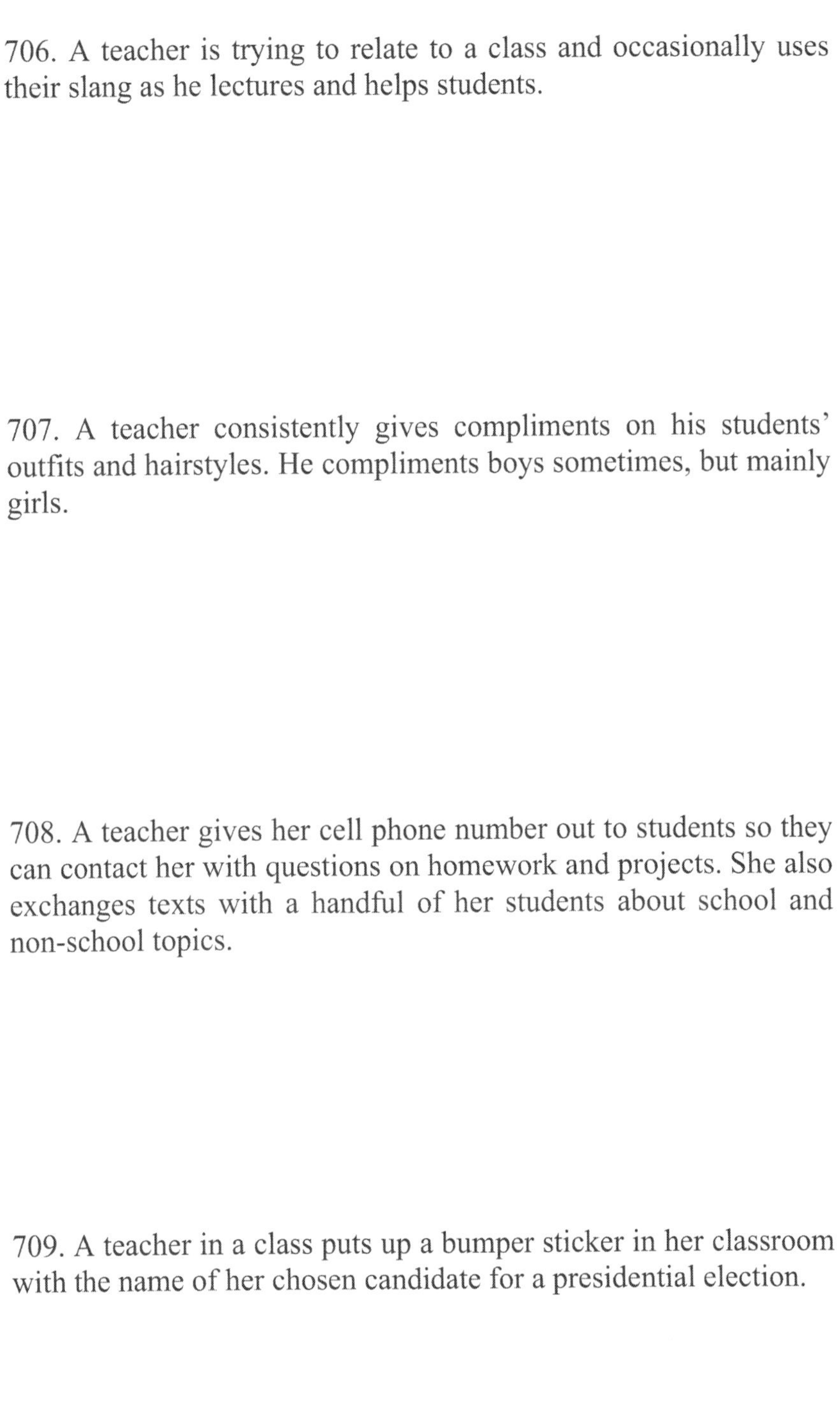

706. A teacher is trying to relate to a class and occasionally uses their slang as he lectures and helps students.

707. A teacher consistently gives compliments on his students' outfits and hairstyles. He compliments boys sometimes, but mainly girls.

708. A teacher gives her cell phone number out to students so they can contact her with questions on homework and projects. She also exchanges texts with a handful of her students about school and non-school topics.

709. A teacher in a class puts up a bumper sticker in her classroom with the name of her chosen candidate for a presidential election.

710. A teacher occasionally recounts self-deprecating and funny stories about his dating life to his class. Would your opinion change if the teacher were openly LGBT?

Colleagues

711. A team of "course-alike" teachers has a common test to be taken in one period without notes. A newer teacher on that team doesn't feel like she has done a great job teaching a particular unit so she gives the students two periods to take the test.

What if she lets them use notes? What if she let them take the test with partners?

712. A veteran teacher says, "Whether they learn or not, I still get paid the same."

713. A teacher enjoys talking about the personal lives of other teachers.

Policy

714. A teacher has a strict policy about late work. He has a good relationship with a particular student who tends to have emotional difficulties and gives that student extra time to turn in most assignments. He does not give this opportunity to other students.

715. A teacher knows that one of her students is trying to maintain his straight-A average as he finishes his senior year. After toiling all of first semester in a class that was difficult for him, he ended up with an 89.4%. The teacher normally rounds up only when the grade is 89.5 and above, but makes an exception for this student.

Would your opinion change if the straight-A student did not try very hard and ended up with an 89.4? What about a kid who almost got a B or almost passed the class?

Professional

716. A teacher has a big test planned and knows that students will be coming the morning of the test for extra help. But something happens and that teacher arrives right at the beginning of class. The students who came in for help are demanding that the teacher move the test back so they can get help. The teacher gives the test that period anyway.

717. A teacher has a student who consistently does not listen to directions. One day after giving directions, the student asks a question that was clearly explained already. The teacher refuses to answer the student, and says that he already explained what to do.

718. A teacher has a good relationship with one of his male students who is a star athlete. The student often has impulsive behavior that lands him in trouble. The student is slated to go to college on a scholarship and is trying to stay out of trouble. The teacher has noticed that the boy has a flirtatious relationship with a girl but sometimes he pushes it too far. One day the boy approaches the girl and smacks her butt. She's upset and walks out of the room but comes back soon afterwards saying that she overreacted. The teacher is initially inclined to report what happened to the dean but knows the student will likely have an out-of-school suspension that will endanger his scholarship and college future. The girl is no longer upset, and the boy apologized to her. The teacher decides to not report the incident.

719. A teacher in a class of only Christians decorates his class for Christmas and talks about Christmas a few times, including the religious reason for the holiday. Would your opinion change if the class had non-Christian students?

720. A teacher likes to instruct the class while sitting on the front table (instead of standing or sitting on a chair). Does it make any difference if a male or female uses this informal style?

721. A teacher is way behind on grading because of events in his personal life. He decides to take a break and shows the students a movie over a period of days that's tangentially related to the subject matter so he can get some grading done.

Would your opinion change if the teacher just called in sick for a few days to get the grading done?

722. A teacher occasionally swears in front of the class to make an emphatic point.

723. A teacher has a good relationship with a student but has been increasingly disappointed with the student's behavior. It seems to be getting worse instead of improving. They talk often about the struggles the student is having but the teacher doesn't feel like he's getting through to her. One day after the student comes into class scantily clad and yelling the f-word at somebody in the hallway, he decides to try a new tactic, and pulls her aside to talk about her actions. The teacher tells the girl that although he believes that she has great potential, she has been acting lately like she is "trash."

Professional

724. At lunch in the faculty cafe, a teacher makes fun of the ways that her students spell and pronounce their names.

725. At lunch in the faculty cafe, a teacher chastises her peers for complaining too much.

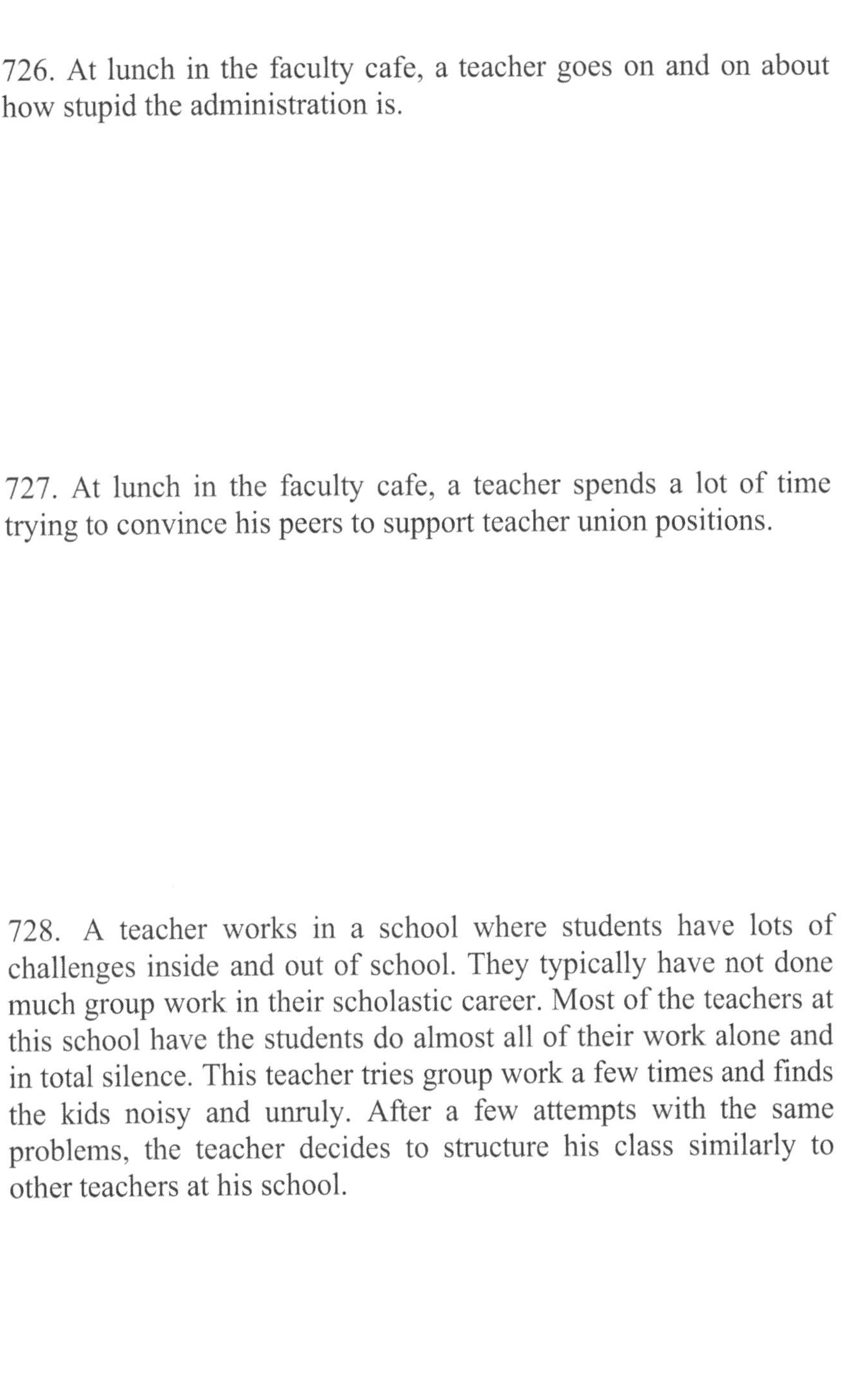

726. At lunch in the faculty cafe, a teacher goes on and on about how stupid the administration is.

727. At lunch in the faculty cafe, a teacher spends a lot of time trying to convince his peers to support teacher union positions.

728. A teacher works in a school where students have lots of challenges inside and out of school. They typically have not done much group work in their scholastic career. Most of the teachers at this school have the students do almost all of their work alone and in total silence. This teacher tries group work a few times and finds the kids noisy and unruly. After a few attempts with the same problems, the teacher decides to structure his class similarly to other teachers at his school.

729. A teacher is assigned a lower-level track in the subject she teaches. One of the first discoveries the teacher makes is that the homework completion rate of her students is very low. Moreover, the points she has assigned to the homework category mean that students who don't often do their homework have significantly lower grades regardless of their performance in other categories (like tests and projects). After a semester, the teacher drops the homework category entirely and eliminates homework.

730. A teacher has a student who is consistently unfocused and resists doing work whenever there is time to do it in class. Just about every day, the teacher goes over to try to convince the student to use her time wisely. As a result of the girl's inaction, she is in danger of failing the course. The teacher tries talking to the girl's guidance counselor and parents on multiple occasions and that doesn't lead to a change in behavior. Midway through the year, the teacher stops trying to motivate the girl to do work because he feels that he has done enough.

Personal Philosophy

731. A teacher grew up in a family where people often spoke using double negatives and using non-standard English words like, "ain't." As a teacher she continues to use double negatives, the word, "ain't," and other non-standard grammar.

732. A teacher in a non-English class believes that it is important for students to always speak in "Standard" English so that they have as many opportunities in life as possible. In this teacher's class are students who speak Black Vernacular English, and students who are English language learners. Every time students make a mistake, the teacher corrects them publicly or privately.

Does the race or language background of the teacher affect your opinion?

733. A teacher knows that a student is involved in gangs but doesn't talk to the school counselor or administrator about it because the problem is so pervasive. In late fall, the student is murdered in a drive-by shooting. The teacher blames herself for the student's death.

What if the teacher did not have any feelings about what happened?

734. When talking to friends on the weekend, a teacher describes his students as idiots.

Chapter 8

Difficult Choices

The education profession is quite susceptible to fads - the self-esteem movement, open space schools, and a focus on multiple intelligences have all come and gone after proving to be ineffective and sometimes hurtful. While medicine, physics and even psychology may similarly change with the times, their respective directions are generally forward. Education, on the other hand, can be quite circular (Being a physics teacher, I might describe it better as oscillatory motion like a pendulum). As a new teacher, I never understood the bitterness exuded by veteran teachers on institute days. However, after only ten years in the profession, I understood their exasperation. In that time, I had already seen initiatives come and go.

I can't predict what will happen with most current educational trends, though I hope the emphasis on teacher learning teams continues. Individual groups have different goals, but the teams tend to focus on improving student learning and using data to improve instruction. Often this means creating common assessments and curricular materials. One drawback is that this process is problematic for teachers accustomed to an individual approach, and even like-minded teachers can struggle for consensus. As hard as this is, I have seen great results from creating and analyzing common materials together. When comparing multiple classrooms and hundreds of students, the trends that arise in student achievement and failure have more statistical strength. It's informative to know that others are having the same problem, and it's helpful to try interventions with some sort of control group.

This collaborative process can be difficult because the manner in which we teach is an extension of ourselves. We can all agree that we want our students to learn; the question of *how* to enhance that process challenges the tenets our teaching values and assumptions about students. Issues as small as what font to use on shared documents can elicit a wide range of opinions. Do you use Comic Sans because students may be more likely to read it or a hard-to-read font because a study showed that students are more likely to remember it? Or do you just use your favorite font because you think it looks the best? I use Times New Roman for the latter reason and can't tolerate comic sans because it looks so childish. With every decision, I have to grapple with whether my personal preference interferes with my capacity to do what is in the best interests of my students.

Other disagreements arise over our assumptions about students. Do we believe that they are doing everything they can to prepare for tests? Where does our responsibility end and theirs begin? Do they need scaffolding for notes or do they need to learn how to do it themselves? If teachers are ordered to create common curricula and tests, how much should they be able to deviate in their presentation of the material? If a teacher does provide more support (for example, giving a practice test nearly identical to the common test), do her students' test results have the same meaning if other teachers offer different practice tests or no practice at all?

During these debates, you'll have to evaluate your various priorities. The first negotiation is between your students and yourself: what works for them and what works for you? The second negotiation is with your colleagues: how much are you willing to compromise and feel that the course is still reflective of what you know to be best for you and your students?

• • •

The last struggle is internal. Let's say that I choose my preference over my students' -- can I justify it? When it comes to font selection, I don't feel very conflicted about making the determination myself. However, other issues are more complex and subtle. I certainly can let my students do corrections on tests because I'm willing to put in the time to regrade work. The issue is whether allowing students to do corrections is ultimately helpful for their learning and test-taking skills. If some students have schedules and responsibilities that don't allow for retakes, am I being equitable in offering this opportunity? If only the students already doing well take advantage of retests, can I argue that this policy is helping underperforming students? Finally, if students always know that they get a second chance, am I reducing the incentive to try hard the first time?

The other half of this internal struggle is deciding when and if I'm going to deviate from the consensus of my team. For example, if the team decides that we are NOT allowing students to retake or correct exams, should I still do it? How strong should I feel about a decision or course of action in order to risk undermining or alienating my colleagues?

For this section, I didn't want teachers in the scenarios to have any distinguishing features so I cycled through the phone book for last names in alphabetical order.

Difficult Choices. Do you agree more with one teacher or another? Why?

Personal Philosophy

801. When students get questions/ideas wrong during class discussions, Mr. Ladner usually tells them that they "were close" (even if they really weren't).

When students get questions/ideas wrong during class discussions, Mr. Macon tells them that they were wrong.

When students get questions/ideas wrong during class discussions, Mrs. Nash tailors her response to each student. For students whose egos can handle it, she tells them that they were wrong, and for students who are more fragile she tells them they were close to the right answer.

802. Ms. Lafleur would like to help students think through their questions but feels there isn't always time. Sometimes she uses Socratic questioning to get at a student's thinking, and other times she just gives them the answer. Moreover, she likes to tailor her answers to the student. For students who can handle a higher-level answer, she gives it to them. For students who need a more straightforward answer, she gives it to him.

Mrs. Maness feels that you should always use higher-level questioning and answering when working with all student queries regardless of the student.

803. Mrs. Jaeger realizes that he has students with vastly different levels of comprehension in her class. She identifies the kids at both ends of the spectrum and assigns higher-level students to lower-level students.

Mr. Kessler also realizes that he has a wide ability range in his class. He encourages students who "get it" to help those who don't, but doesn't force any conversations.

804. Mr. Ng does group work in class and wants his students to be comfortable and work with their friends (unless this is too much of a distraction).

Mr. Peltier does group work in class and wants the students to be with peers that are outside of their social circles to push their boundaries even if it means they are less comfortable.

Mr. Quigley does group work in class and wants students to be with peers with whom they don't get along so that they learn conflict resolution.

Mr. Rodriguez randomly assigns partners and groups to avoid accusations of bias and because in the real world, you can't pick your work colleagues.

Personal Philosophy

805. Mr. Ames has converted all of his documents into Comic Sans because a study showed that students are more likely to read in that font.

Mr. Betz has converted all of his documents into a harder-to-read font because a study showed that students are more likely to retain the material they have read if they have to work harder to read it.

Mr. Concepcion puts all of his documents into Times New Roman because he likes that font.

806. Mrs. Foster's students tend to not do their assigned reading from the book. She decides to make photocopies in the school duplicating center of all readings and turns them into packets so students don't have to carry their book around.

Mr. Gossett's students also tend not to do their assigned reading in the book. Mr. Gossett chooses not to photocopy the readings because he feels that students should experience the consequences of not using their books instead of being accommodated.

Mrs. Hearn's students also tend not to do their assigned readings in the book, but Mrs. Hearn's school doesn't allow its teachers to make so many copies. She goes to a local copy store to make the packets and pays for them.

807. Mr. Jett and Mr. Kimble both do the same project at the end of a semester. Mr. Jett gives out the information two months in advance so that the students have a lot of time to think about their work. Mr. Kimble gives out the information two weeks in advance so students don't have time to procrastinate.

808. During group work Mrs. Tovar spends a lot of time walking around the classroom, answering questions and keeping kids on task.

During group work Mr. Ulrich makes it known that he is available for help, but largely does not circulate. Moreover, he feels that if students aren't using their time well, that's their choice and will be reflected in lower grades.

809. Mrs. Saavedra is teaching a class that struggles to do well on tests though part of the problem is they don't study enough. After a series of bad test scores, Mrs. Saavedra decides to give the students practice tests ahead of the exam. She also makes the test itself very similar to the practice test so the students feel confident and familiar with the material.

Mr. Treadwell also likes to give practice tests but feels strongly that the test should be noticeably different than the practice test. Mr. Treadwell thinks that Mrs. Saavedra's method rewards memorization rather than true comprehension.

810. Mrs. Valdez has a review day before tests. She makes herself available for student questions but feels like it is the responsibility of the students to prepare and know what they need to ask.

Ms. Wertz has a review day before tests. She prepares materials to help the students figure out what they know and what they don't know. She prepares a lesson that reviews the material and answers questions if they come up.

Mrs. Wu does not have a review day before tests. She prepares materials to help the students figure out what they know and what they don't know. She makes the answers available online and expects the students to come in before or after school if they need help.

811. Mr. York starts class the second the bell rings. He says this helps make the most of the period.

Mr. Zimmer starts class with some informal conversations with the class. After five to ten minutes, he begins the lesson. He feels this brings him closer to his students and helps them to begin the period more focused.

812. Mrs. Coon tells students explicitly what to write down in their notes so that they have what they need for the tests.

Mr. Dengle has the students take notes but asks them to figure out what they should write down.

Ms. Earl writes skeleton notes where the students fill in the blank so they can focus on the ideas rather than writing so much.

Mr. Friedman prints up all of his notes and distributes them to students so they can give all of their attention to the ideas of the lesson.

Professional

813. Mr. Archibald works in a school that has a strict dress code which includes not wearing hats. Mr. Archibald feels like the policy creates friction between him and his students. He allows students to wear hats so everyone is comfortable.

Mr. Bernstein believes that Mr. Archibald is making it more difficult for other teachers in the school to enforce the policy and is "buying" the affection of the students through a lax implementation of school policy.

814. Mr. Espinosa tends to dress very casually in a school that doesn't have an official dress code for teachers. Students sometimes remark that he is dressed like he's hanging out on the weekend, but Mr. Espinosa says that it makes him and his students more relaxed and ready to learn.

Mr. Fife feels that the clothes that Mr. Espinosa wears to school denigrates the profession and leads to less respect in the eyes of students.

Would your opinion change if the casually dressed teacher was female?

815. Mr. Gillie is very active on Facebook and posts statuses just about every day. Sometimes the posts are about his personal life and sometimes they are about his job as a teacher. Some of the teaching-related posts are about positive experiences and some are negative ones, particularly about difficult interactions with students. Some of the posts are about negative experiences, and some are genuine attempts to seek advice from his teacher friends while others are just rants.

Mrs. Haynes is also active on Facebook but never posts about teaching. She thinks it's unprofessional and worries that Mr. Gillie's posts (regardless of who can see them) could be misinterpreted and lead to parent complaints or disciplinary action.

816. Mr. Quinn wants his students to do as well as possible and knows that some students can't come after or before school for help. In addition to being available before and after school, he organizes a study session at a local restaurant the night before the test.

Mr. Rogers doesn't like that Mr. Quinn is going beyond his contractual obligations to the school and students while creating a liability issue. Mr. Rogers also worries that Mr. Quinn is blurring the lines between being a teacher and being a friend.

Class Policy

817. Mr. Cohn has a strict policy for turning in late assignments; they are never allowed. It's either there the day it's due or there's no credit.

Mr. Delacruz feels that Mr. Cohn's policy is too harsh and doesn't allow for the various unforeseen events that occur in the lives of young people.

818. Mrs. Knapp teaches seniors and one day a student asks her for a recommendation. However, the student had procrastinated and the recommendation was due the next day. Mrs. Knapp tells the student that it was a big request, but feels bad for the student and writes the recommendation that evening at home.

Mr. Juarez believes that Mrs. Knapp should have refused the student request because it was an unfair imposition, and because it teaches the students that they can procrastinate and still get what they want.

819. Ms. Armstrong and Mr. Blackburn both teach an honors class that moves at a fast pace. Mrs. Armstrong feels that the volume of content warrants tests on material covered in class and material that was assigned but not covered in class. Mr. Blackburn feels that it is fair to only test on material covered in class, even though that means less total material.

820. Mrs. Nesbitt notices that some of her students do poorly on exams and is worried that the final exam will further lower their grades. She designs a group project that is worth half of the students' final exam grade in order to reward the students who work hard, but don't test well.

Mrs. Peralta says that it is dangerous to have a group project worth so much. If there is a person who doesn't do their part, it could drastically affect the grade of the other group members and lead to other problems.

821. Ms. Romano has her students do make-up tests during class to get them done as soon as possible.

Ms. Spencer has her students schedule make-up tests outside of class so that they never miss instructional time.

822. Mr. Upton assigns homework and gives students credit based on completion. Mr. Upton feels that it would be too stressful to assign points for correctness and wants the students to have an opportunity to practice the new material. The students go over the answers together in class.

Mr. Varner corrects the homework that is assigned. Mr. Varner feels that the students only take the homework seriously if there are points attached to correct answers. Mr. Varner goes over the homework after it is graded.

Ms. Washington assigns homework but does not correct it or give points for it. Ms. Washington gives the students an opportunity to ask questions in class but feels that the students should only get credit for showing their understanding on tests.

823. Mr. Tracey plays music that the students pick during activities. Mr. Tracey feels that it contributes to a warmer atmosphere where the students feel comfortable.

Ms. Yu does not play music in class. Ms. Yu finds the music that students like to be pretty objectionable and worries that although many students work better with music playing, it adversely affects other students.

Mrs. Zimmerman plays music in class that she likes and does not take student requests.

824. Ms. Dougherty noticed that sometimes her students forget to turn a sheet over and respond to the questions on the back. To fix this, she puts a little text box on every double-sided sheet saying, "turn over, please."

Mr. Eaves also has students who forget to look at the backside. She chooses not to add any special text because students should know to check the backside of a sheet.

825. Mrs. Ledesma and Mr. Merchant make copies of a packet for a multiday unit. Mrs. Ledesma makes 15% more than she needs because some students lose theirs and need replacements. Mr. Merchant makes just enough because he feels that if students lose their packets, they should experience the natural consequence.

826. Mrs. Haas tries to figure out as soon as possible if a student is in the right level of a course. If she feels that the student has been misplaced, she counsels them to change levels (usually down).

Mr. Irving lets students figure out for themselves if they are in the correct class and level. He responds to student and parent questions about level changes, but never initiates the conversation.

827. After experiencing the death of a student in his class, Mr. Meade immediately rearranges the seating chart so that students don't have to become saddened by looking at the empty seat of the student who passed.

After experiencing the death of a student in his class, Mrs. Griffith keeps the dead student's desk empty. Students are allowed to leave notes and pictures on it.

828. Mr. Edwards, Ms. Rummel and Mrs. Price all teach 1st period classes with lower-level students who struggle to get to class on time. Despite various school-wide interventions, on a given day there may be five to ten missing students.

Mr. Edwards waits a few minutes to officially begin class. He fills this time by talking with the students and catching up on their lives.

Ms. Rummel starts class immediately when the bell rings. If students come in late, he feels that it is their loss.

Mrs. Price starts each class with a quick quiz. If the students come in late, they miss the quiz and that adversely affects their grades.

829. Ms. Martinez, Mr. Prichard, Ms. Dorsey, and Mrs. Steele struggle with students who are absent and neglect to make up their work. All of them have old assignments available in the classroom.

Ms. Martinez does nothing special for missing students. She expects them to ask a peer what they missed and get the assignment for themselves.

Mr. Prichard posts assignments online. She expects students to check the assignments on the web.

Ms. Dorsey pulls aside students when they return to discuss what they missed. They are still expected to grab the assignments they missed and copy the notes from a peer.

Mrs. Steele pulls aside students when they return and hands them the missing assignments and a copy of the notes.

Chapter 9

Conclusion

There is no shortage of books on teaching that will claim to tell you what works to better educate students and manage classrooms. The problem is that these books cannot impart all of the possible approaches and strategies that will be effective specifically for you and your students. The focus of this book has been determining who you are in relation to your students; that requires a much deeper sense of self-awareness and understanding of your students' needs. What works for one teacher won't necessarily work for another, and what works for one class of students may not work for the next. Most importantly, what works for you at the start of your career may be different than what works when you are a mature educator. "What works" is not a static list of techniques that can be enshrined in a book, but an ever changing cache of methods that depend on both the educator and those to be educated.

Ultimately, educational history and theory as well as, national, state, and school policy exist move to the periphery as educators struggle to make countless small and large decisions on how to be true to themselves and still be most helpful to their students. There's a movement to have administrators do more observations, particularly short "walk-throughs," but most of the time, it will be just you and your students. In fact, current fire code mandates that your door be closed at all times, furthering your isolation. Theory, school policy and contractual obligations often have to be interpreted at the spur of the moment with students watching every move you make. They notice mistakes, contradictions, and openings for manipulation but also positive examples of what can be done under duress. The process of students defying teachers (and their parents) is ubiquitous, and you have to pass their examinations as much as they have to pass yours.

I have argued in this book that it is a mistake to believe in one solution for any given problem. Instead, teachers have to grapple with the myriad multi-level challenges that express themselves as tensions between many justifiable paths. Do we treat our students like growing children or young adults? Do we stick exclusively to the material in our curriculum or do we help them with the prerequisite skills that they should have already mastered? Do we focus purely on academics or do we address the social emotional realm with the goal of improving their ability to concentrate on the subject matter? When do our jobs end and our personal lives begin? Or should we live for our jobs?

No matter what you choose and where you compromise, it's important to have well thought out reasons for your actions. Only through continual reflection coupled with constructive feedback from colleagues and students can you develop your own decision-making process. Establishing a coherent and personalized system for making decisions as a teacher is a career-long challenge that's commonly underestimated. It is important to remember that even a highly evolved and thoughtful teacher won't necessarily be able to effectively teach all of her students. Furthermore, it is no secret that factors outside of the classroom can drastically affect a student's disposition towards learning. Even the most dedicated teacher cannot completely compensate for these outside influences. Moreover, when you personalize your presentation style, there will still be some that benefit more than others. I am reminded of this fact when I read my student evaluations at the end of each year.

For every ten students who thought I provided much needed levity to the subject of physics, there's at least one who considered my style offensive.

Given that the extent of your influence is unknowable, and some students you struggle to engage may ultimately fail, it's fair to wonder what the point of this entire reflective process is. A less committed educator may rationalize failures in the classroom on the basis that things just happened…I tried my best…and that's how it turned out. A more committed, reflective educator can review her systematic efforts to understand and meet her students' needs in order to have a better idea of exactly why certain approaches worked better for a given student or class.

Justifying your choices isn't enough – you'll often have to struggle with the extent to which you choose a path that serves you or your students. For example, if you decide not to distribute a study packet before a test, you may think that the choice forces the students to learn how to study better. However, you'll also have to ask yourself if the real reason is that you just don't feel like making a study packet and the "teaching them to study" argument is a rationalization. If you arrive at the conclusion that it was indeed a rationalization, you then have another series of choices, the worst of which is to punish yourself. Start planning for next year, collaborate with colleagues who teach the same course or even have the students create their own study guide.

Let's say that you find yourself yelling at a particular class or student. Again, you can tell yourself that it's what the class or student needed to hear in order to correct misbehavior, but it's worth wondering whether it's you that has a problem controlling your students or your temper. I have seen teachers struggle on both sides of this issue (yellers who don't know when they have gone too far and accommodators whose personality prevents them from being stern). It could certainly be true that an appropriately timed reprimand improves the learning environment, and it could simultaneously be true you have an issue controlling the volume and tone of your voice. If you are feeling conflicted or confused, you could start recording these outbursts more formally, ask a peer to observe you, or talk to the students directly about what they think helps them stay on task.

A tension that often stymies new teachers is deciding when to be punitive and when to be forgiving for everything from misbehavior to late assignments. Teachers have to balance their own time when it comes to accepting late work and the message that it may send when they apply justice (enforce the rule for late assignments) or show mercy (allow a deviation from the rule). As the previous two examples illustrated, there is still work to be done after you have made and justified a course of action. You can follow up to see if your choice had the desired effect (did the students continue to turn in late assignments?) and reflect on whether you applied your course of action equitably. When it came to showing mercy, who were the recipients? Was it everyone in a similar situation or was it just the students that you knew well? Was it students of all genders or backgrounds, or just the ones that you unconsciously favor?

I predict that your answers to the questions in this book will grow more nuanced as your teaching career develops. You will be able to cite your post-secondary studies, current research in education and your own experience as you hone your abilities to make decisions as a teacher. It sounds like an overwhelmingly complex and confusing challenge, but I believe that the more you understand yourself in relation to your students, the more you can *be* yourself with your students. In fact, once you delve deeply into this reflective process, you'll never have to grumble about going to "work" like so many professionals do. You will have the opportunity to wake up every morning and go to *school* where you can be the version of yourself that is best for you and your students.

Acknowledgements

I want to give special thanks to my father, Mark Podolner, who read all of my first drafts and was somehow able to fill in the spaces between what I wanted to say and what I had written. Melissa Nemeth and Joe Matuch (Team PodoMoJoe) were instrumental in giving me new-teacher and Scholar feedback. Pamela Podolner, my loving wife and partner in creativity, helped in a multitude of ways. My mom, Marion Sirefman, did a great job catching typos and giving advice on the cover.

Golden Apple Scholars LaJoi Royston, Elisabeth Knierem, and Namita Shah were early supporters and reviewers. UIC Alum Keith Mukai helped me remake the introduction to this book. Colleagues Naomi Hildner, Steve Goldberg, Phil Prale, Ben Cain, James Kryger, Allison Myers and Avi Lessing all added their own flavor to this text. Don Duggan-Haas, my former education professor, has always been supportive of my efforts in the classroom. Golden Apple stars Mark Larson, Penny Lundquist, Peg Cain and Dominic Belmonte lent their voices, thoughts and talents to this project.

About The Author

In 2004, at age 25 and during his fourth year of teaching, Aaron S. Podolner became the youngest winner ever of the Chicago-Area Golden Apple Award for Excellence in Education. Since then he has continued to teach physics to a wide range of students at Oak Park and River Forest High School in Oak Park, IL, and every summer he conducts reflective seminars for future teachers through the Golden Apple Scholar of Illinois program.

The Scholars program identifies talented high school seniors and college sophomores who have the promise and drive to be excellent teachers in high-need schools. The Golden Apple Foundation prepares them for immediate and lasting success in some of the most challenging teaching environments. In the fall of 2012, Podolner was named Golden Apple's "Director of Reflection" and now provides guidance for all of the Foundation's reflective seminar leaders.

Podolner lives in a suburb of Chicago with his wife and three young daughters. He can be contacted through the book's website at: www.facebook.com/HowWouldYouHandleIt